T0329448

Debating Witchcraft in Africa
The "Magritte Effect"

Edited by

Didier Péclard
&
Jean Pierre Warnier

Langaa Research & Publishing CIG
Mankon, Bamenda

Publisher
Langaa RPCIG
Langaa Research & Publishing Common Initiative Group
P.O. Box 902 Mankon
Bamenda
North West Region
Cameroon
Langaagrp@gmail.com
www.langaa-rpcig.net

Distributed in and outside N. America by African Books Collective
orders@africanbookscollective.com
www.africanbookscollective.com

ISBN-10: 9956-550-02-7
ISBN-13: 978-9956-550-02-9

Table of contents

iii

Preface

Witchcraft in Africa
Debating the "Magritte Effect"

Didier Péclard
University of Geneva
Co-Editor of *Politique africaine*

In a recent issue of *Politique africaine*, Jean-Pierre Warnier interrogated what he called the "Magritte effect" in the study of witchcraft[1]. Looking back on his 45-year long experience in and with Cameroon, he wondered why he was experiencing a feeling of "cognitive dissonance" with regards to witchcraft. On the one hand, he noted, there has been a flood of publications on the topic over the past thirty years, many of them arguing that witchcraft is a sort of "coat lining" for any human activity. This contrasted starkly with the fact that, on the other hand, during the four decades that he spent sharing "the daily life of hundreds of Cameroonian friends, neighbours and acquaintances" (Warnier, this volume, p.6), he was "the direct witness, without any kind of mediation, of only three witchcraft crises, with their retinue of anxiety, panic, somatic conditions and accusations (p.6).

Drawing on this observation, and without denying the importance of witchcraft as a representation of the real, he encouraged Africanist researchers to take some distance in order to avoid "mistaking the map for the territory, the

---

[1] J.-P. Warnier, "Ceci n'est pas un sorcier. De l'effet Magritte en sorcellerie", *Politique africaine*, n 146, June 2017, p. 125-141.

smoking pipe for the pipe, the narrative for the event, the rumour for the actual crisis" (p.7). He thus called for a "sociology of witchcraft crises" that would help draw "a clear distinction between the real economy, power relationships, social dynamics on the one hand, and the various kinds of verbal constructions on the other hand" (p.24).

These arguments called for a debate. The editorial board of *Politique africaine* therefore invited six Africanist scholars to discuss Warnier's provocative essay[2]. This book is the English version of the whole debate, with Warnier's original piece, contributions from Julien Bonhomme, Patrice Yengo, Jane Guyer, Joseph Tonda, Francis Nyamnjoh, Peter Geschiere and a response by the author of the "Magritte effect".

Politique africaine has a long history of engaging with the issue of witchcraft. A rapid search in the journal's archives[3] with keywords such as "sorcellerie", "sorcier" or "invisible" gives well over 250 occurrences. Any attempt at providing a comprehensive review of these articles would be foolhardy and not necessarily relevant. Instead, let me underline three aspects which I would argue run through most of these contributions.

First, witchcraft, or the "invisible" dimension of the exercise of power in African societies was in many ways at the heart of the epistemological project out of which *Politique africaine* was born. It was one of the many expressions of the "politics from below"[4] which the journal set out to focus on in order to provide an alternative perspective on African societies

---

[2] D. Péclard (coord.), "Sorcellerie en Afrique: 'L'effet Magritte' en débat", *Politique africaine*, n 148, December 2017, p. 131-168.

[3] See <http://www.politique-africaine.com/> for issues 1 to 72 and <https://www.cairn.info/revue-politique-africaine.htm> for issues 73 onwards.

[4] See for instance: J.-F. Bayart, "Le politique par le bas en Afrique noire. Questions de méthode", *Politique africaine*, n 1, March 1981, p. 53-82.

and polities, away from the narratives of crisis[5] that dominated (and still largely dominate) the study of Africa. Second, most authors seem to agree on the polysemic and multidimensional character of the variegated social dynamics generally grouped under the term "witchcraft" – a term which, as many authors including in the present volume note, is often very ill-suited to translate this extremely elusive object. As Florence Bernault and Joseph Tonda note in the introduction to the special issue they coordinated on "*pouvoirs sorciers*", witchcraft can be used in the same social group simultaneously as a "social equalizer" and a "tool for economic and political accumulation"[6].

The third, and arguably most discussed topic that runs through these contributions is the question of modernity. While the modernist *Zeitgeist* of the post-independence period had led some to predict the "decline of superstitions" in the face of "economic development, urban life, written culture and monotheist religions"[7], it is its impressive vitality that forced the question of witchcraft onto the research agenda of the late 1980s and 1990s. How to interpret this enduring vitality? Peter Geschiere, one of the main voices on the issue[8], summarized the terms of the debate in the following manner: seeing witchcraft as an expression of modernity, on the one hand,

---

[5] A. Mbembe, "Pouvoir, violence et accumulation", *Politique africaine*, n 39, October 1990, p. 7-24.

[6] F. Bernault and J. Tonda, "Dynamiques de l'invisible en Afrique", *Politique africaine*, n 79, October 2000, p. 5-16.

[7] *Ibid.*, p. 5

[8] P. Geschiere, *Sorcellerie et politique en Afrique. La viande des autres*, Paris, Karthala, 1995 (translated as *The Modernity of Witchcraft*, University of Virginia Press, 197). See also P. Geschiere, *Witchcraft, Intimacy and Trust. Africa in Comparison*, Chicago/London, The University of Chicago Press, 2013, and the debate published on this book in *Politique africaine*, with contributions from Robert Muchembled, Mathieu Salpeteur et Joseph Tonda (*Politique africaine*, n 135, 2014, p. 197-224).

provides "a strategic entry point to conceive the complexity of modernity as such", while also pointing at "the enduring importance of secrecy as essential to any form of power". On the other hand, it "helps disentangle witchcraft from a-historical 'traditions' and better perceive the innovative creativity of these representations"[9].

Undoubtedly, like many other Africanist journals and publishers, *Politique africaine* has contributed to the successive waves of publications on witchcraft which were the starting point for Warnier's feeling of "cognitive dissonance". The contributions in the following pages allow the discussion to move one step further by discussing three main questions: (1) How can researchers distinguish, as Warnier urges them to do, between *discourses* and *practices* or *experiences* on and of witchcraft? Is it heuristically possible – and even desirable? (2) What are the methodological biases which contribute to the "Magritte effect" and how can they be avoided? (3) What are the conditions of possibility for the development of a "sociology of witchcraft crises" that would help generate a more precise knowledge, both quantitative and qualitative, of the importance and the role of witchcraft in contemporary African (and other) societies?

These questions, and others addressed by the authors, cannot possibly be answered in all their complexity in just a few dozen pages. We hope however that they will contribute to renewing the debate around this resolutely elusive and yet extremely "real" object.

I would like to thank Karthala, the publisher of *Politique africaine*, for authorizing the English publication, Francis Nyamnjoh for taking the initiative of the English publication

---

[9] P. Geschiere, "Sorcellerie et modernité: retour sur une étrange complicité", *Politique africaine*, n 79, October 2000, p. 32.

and making it happen, Moshumee Teena Dewoo for translating the texts into English, and of course Jean-Pierre Warnier for triggering the debate in the first place and the six contributors for pursuing it.

PART I

"This Is Not a Witch. About the Magritte Effect in Matters of Witchcraft"

Jean-Pierre Warnier

Imaf (Institut des mondes africains), Paris

As a witness to the conference "Witchcraft and Justice" organized in 2005 in Yaoundé by Eric de Rosny[1], Alban Bensa raised an unsettling question: "could it be that the conference contributed to legitimizing the discourse of/on witchcraft and "give a scholarly label to it?"[2]. I wish to go one step further: given the circularity of the witchcraft complex in Africa, given its performative potential, isn't the flood of anthropological publications on the topic counter-productive insofar as it feeds what it pretends to analyse, and even stigmatize[3]? P. Geschiere goes so far as to write that the fight conducted by Cameroonian courts and Pentecostal churches has also had such an adverse effect.

I have been asking that very question over the last few years. I have come to the conclusion that, as an anthropologist,

---

[1] E. de Rosny (ed.), *Justice et sorcellerie*, Paris, Karthala, 2006.

[2] A. Bensa, "La sorcellerie: un imaginaire du pouvoir", in E. de Rosny (ed.), *Justice et sorcellerie, op. cit.* p. 342.

[3] The bibliography is so considerable that it is impossible to do justice to it. Let us quote only three recent titles that condense the latest discussions: P. Yengo, *Les mutations sorcières dans le basin du Congo. Du ventre et de sa politique*, Paris, Karthala, 2016; P. Geschiere, *Witchcraft, Intimacy and Trust. Africa in Comparison*, Chicago, The University of Chicago Press, 2013; E. Galland, *Figures et imaginaires de la réussite sociale à Yaoundé. Les enjeux moraux d'un débat public*, these de doctorat en anthropologie, Université d'Aix-Marseille, 2016.

I would be well advised to be more careful, to stop emulating Pentecostal preachers, and to avoid bestowing on Africa the dubious privilege of being no more than a shadow-theatre devoid of substance or seriousness on which everything – power, work, production, economy – would actually be played in the occult. My colleagues in the social sciences will judge for themselves by considering the following arguments.

First of all I wish to suggest under what circumstances this question became more urgent. Of recent, current academic life has played its part. Indeed, Emmanuel Galland[4] has recently submitted a remarkable doctoral dissertation devoted to the imaginary of social success in Yaoundé, and on the moral stakes of the public debates thereof in which discourses and representations concerning the occult feature prominently, to such an extent that, if they are to be believed, any social practice whatever appears to the eyes of the actors as a box with a false bottom. At face value, one can see civil servants of the National Assembly, young women, prominent men and urban youth (the four categories that E. Galland considers as "strategic" ones) who crave for personal achievement and wonder about the required conditions for its realization. If his enquiries are anything to come by, being grounded in interviews and verbal comments, his informants are of the opinion that success and failure are also achieved in the occult, to such an extent that people view those activities as a shadow-theatre the truth of which is located behind the stage, in the remote worlds of witchcraft and sorcery that define what E. Galland calls a moral economy. Beyond the four categories identified by the author, one may expect that many actors not mentioned by him – the taxi driver, trader, transporter,

---

4 E. Galland, *Figures et imaginaires de la réussite, op, cit.*

4

mechanic, carpenter – are equally confronted to the constraints of the occult world.

His ethnographic rendering is so faithful to the vernacular language of his informants – the 'camfranglais' – and to the urban scenery, to the actors and places, that it transports me straight away into the Yaoundé urban quarters where I lived for several years. And yet, I do not quite find my bearings. Concerning witchcraft/sorcery, I suffer from a cognitive gap. In the Cameroon I know and am used to, the witchcraft crisis is one of the many contingencies of daily life, just as traffic accidents in the streets of Paris, that, for most people, impact only from far away their pragmatic conduct. By contrast, if E. Galland is to be believed, the people of Yaoundé have a representation of their environment and speak about it as a mixed entity, a world in which any practical activity would have a lining, like that of a coat. In that respect, the role played by the media would be crucial, and E. Galland[5] quotes Henry and Tall who claim that: "the media contribute to spread and turn into something banal an imaginary of witchcraft, to turn it into something credible that is confirmed by the authority enjoyed by the press." There is no doubt that the supply provided by the media is precisely that one. No one would challenge that. However, does the public take it at face value? Can we infer from the journalistic provision system to the reception, and presume of the capacity of the readers and audience for critique and mockery[6].

---

[5] Ibid., p. 125 ; C. Henry et K. Tall, "La sorcellerie envers et contre tous", *Cahiers d'études africaines*, n° 189-190, 2008, pp. 11-34.

[6] Concerning the broadcasting of witchcraft by the media and its reception, see the publications by J. Bonhomme, *Les voleurs de sexe: anthropologie d'une rumeur africaine*, Paris, Seuil, 2009; "La sorcellerie à l'heure des medias", *in* S. Fancello (dir), *Penser la sorcellerie en Afrique*, Paris, Hermann, 2015, p. 83-116.

About the Magritte effect in the case of witchcraft

By contrast, my own experience recommends being more careful. I made a number of visits to Cameroon ever since 1971. Consolidated together, they amount to some ten full years (short periods of leave set aside) – three years as a researcher living at the outskirts of Bamenda and seven years in Yaoundé as a university lecturer. At the time, I was staying around Chapelle d'Obili – a popular urban quarter. Moreover, my partner at the time stayed three more years with our child. Consequently, I returned there at every short vacation and I kept in touch with the daily life of our friends and colleagues in town and at the university. Subsequently, I returned there quite regularly, including a four months stay in 2002. My last visit dates back to 2009. Altogether, it amounts to 45 years of contact and at least 15 years of close proximity, of which 10 as a resident.

During all those years I shared the daily life of hundreds of Cameroonian friends, neighbours and acquaintances. Yet I have been the direct witness, without any kind of mediation, of only three witchcraft crises, with their retinue of anxiety, panic, somatic conditions and accusations. I call witchcraft crisis a climactic episode during which a clearly identified subject becomes convinced, with the support of his entourage, that s/he has fallen victim to a witchcraft/sorcery attack. The ethnographic method makes it possible to distinguish between such an event on the one hand, and suspicions, fears, rumours, gossips, background media noise, anthropological publications that are witness to a generalized belief in witchcraft in Africa, and that I call witchcraft representations, without further discrimination, although it would be necessary to introduce them. Marc Augé[7] has made a step in that direction when he introduced a distinction between a suspicion and an accusation of witchcraft that – thought he – the Manchester school had tended to play down. P. Geschiere[8] went one step further in his critique by integrating witchcraft/sorcery into the overall social order, as an obscure and ambiguous component of it.

Collapsing together the crisis and its representations amounts to yield to what I call the Magritte effect, that is, to mistaking the map for the territory, the painting of the smoking pipe for the pipe, the narrative for the event, the rumour for the actual crisis. Publications on witchcraft in Africa seem to yield to this bias more often than not. I can sense the objection: the painting by Magritte and the smoking pipe are tangible objects[9]. They can be easily told from one another since their affordance is not the same: one can stuff tobacco into the pipe, lit it, bring its beak to one's mouth and smoke. This cannot be done with the painting. By contrast, the witch cannot be grasped by any other means than the rumour and the discourse that surround his deeds. Is it so true? Obviously, witchcraft is something that all observers agree to underscore its polymorphism and its inscription in complex forms of linguistic expressions. Consequently, I only speak of the Magritte effect as an analogy that should not be taken at face value. In any case, it is worth a debate, with possibly a heuristic surplus value that may be worth considering.

No doubt, one can seldom meet with a witch, only when he confesses his misdeeds (and even so is there any such thing

---

[7] M. Augé, *Théorie des pouvoirs et idéologie. Etude de cas en Côte d'Ivoire*, Paris, Hermann, 1975.

[8] P. Geschiere, *Sorcellerie et politique en Afrique. La viande des autres*, Paris, Karthala, 1995.

[9] On the Magritte effect, see J.-P. Warnier. *The Pot-King. The Body and Technologies of power*, Leiden, Boston: Brill, 2007: 5-6.

as a real witch even when he states he is one?), in such a way that the discourse on/by witchcraft is almost the only thing that one can investigate. Yet, between the witch and the narratives that keep circulating among the public, there is a tangible element that can be substantiated. That is, the witchcraft crisis that hits a subject, reaches him through his body or his belongings, releases on his entourage a flood of anxiety and even panic, and triggers a sequence in which bodily conducts combine with performative speech, with narratives, and with the use of material objects and substances involved in the treatment. This tangible event provides the mirror image of the elusive witch. We are clearly confronted with three distinct elements: a tangible witchcraft crisis around a clearly identified subject, the representations of the said crisis, or of witchcraft generally speaking – let us say the words uttered on/by witchcraft – and the always elusive witch. All the conditions are met for us to mistake the discourse/representations for the crisis, the painting for the smoking pipe, and to yield to the Magritte effect[10]

Three cases of witchcraft attacks

This is the ethnographic account of the only three cases that I could observe as a direct, first-hand, witness in 45 years, beginning with the less fine grain account to the more detailed

---

[10] J. Bonhomme has been kind enough to provide me with a critical assessment of this article before its publication, in which he suggests to draw a distinction between three elements: 1) the general discourses on witchcraft, routinely produced by the public; 2) the narratives about witchcraft that circulate, that are the object of extensive comments; and 3) the narratives in which the narrator or his immediate entourage is personally involved (that I call the crisis). Such distinctions bring a useful light on the debate and bring some qualifications on my analyses.

one. The first two are reduced to the bare essentials. In 1974, Anye' (pseudonym), a farmer in Bamenda, fell victim to a household accident that caused third degree burns. He was admitted in emergency at the Bamenda hospital where he died three days later of his wounds. His nephew, emotionally very upset, informed me that Anye' had engaged in a trading partnership with two men who attracted him into very lucrative transactions. Anye' soon suspected that they were unwholesome ones. He decided to break clean of them. It was too late. The two men belonged to what is known as *ngang minang bashie* in Mbam-Nkam languages ("those [of the] secret [of the] ground"), the equivalent of the Bamileke *famla'* and of the Duala *ekong*[11]. One evening, they paid a visit to Anye' in order to claim their due in members of his kin group. The meeting turned sour. His family, whom I know well, is overwhelmed with anxiety. His kin are convinced that, because he refused to deliver one or more parents to the gang members, he was compelled to sacrifice his own life. He is now believed to be kept in slavery and to work in occult plantations on the slopes of the Manenguba Mountain, and to enrich his prosecutors.

I have never met Anye'. By contrast, in the second case, I have met Oyono (pseudonym) for a long time. I know him personally. He is the chief mechanic of a garage employing about thirty workers where my partner and I used to have our car repaired and maintained. One day in 1983, the garage

---

[11] This form of witchcraft, known as "envoûtement" in francophone Cameroon, is grounded in an imaginary translation of the slave trade, of slavery, and of forced labour in the plantations under colonization: a person disappears, and, subsequently, somebody in his entourage is found to have acquired riches the origin of which cannot be explained. This imaginary combines with that of a rotating credit association between slave-dealers and those who take advantage of the trade.

director, who is a friend of us, and a neighbour in Obili quarter, tells us that he feels concerned about Oyono. The latter finds it more and more difficult to walk. A diagnosis of *ekong* (or "envoûtement") falls some time later. I pay a visit to the garage. The anxiety is tangible. The director keeps us informed once in a while. Oyono is being cured by a traditional healer who validates his suspicions. In three months' time, the chief mechanic recovers his full bodily motions. I do not know if the author of the attack has been identified.

The third case is somewhat better documented than the other two. I will describe it into more details. It dates back to 1983. John (pseudonym) is one of my colleagues at the University of Yaoundé where he has been teaching for over fifteen years. He has a doctorate degree ("Doctorat d'Etat") of the University of Paris and occupies a full professorship. We both teach in the same programs. Back from summer leave in the first days of September, I meet him in the corridors of the Faculty building. I approach him, ready for an embrace, but he stops me short of it by propping both hands, palms opened, raised in front of him. He sweats profusely. He exhibits his swollen hands, says he suffers from an oedema, and says that laboratory analyses have not detected anything wrong with him. I translate mentally by a diagnosis of witchcraft/sorcery attack.

During the following week, John does not show up, even once, at the University. I feel worried about him and call on his wife Joséphine (pseudonym) at her work place. We know each other quite well. I ask her about John. She does not commit herself. I do not insist. A week later, it is her turn to call on me, in the late afternoon, at my home. She informs me that John has fallen victim to *ekong* ("envoûtement"). He is under treatment with a healer a few kilometres away from Yaoundé where he has settled down. He requests my visit.

The very next day in the afternoon, I call at the hamlet of the practitioner. It is a group of a dozen raw bricks buildings with corrugated aluminium or thatch roofs. In the courtyard, a few patients attend to the preparation of their meal or to daily chores. The healer – a *nganga* – has been informed of my visit and welcomes me. He leads me to the hut of a dozen square metres in which I find John. He is lying on a bed. In front of the *nganga*, John gives me a detailed account of what had happened to him. One month earlier, he paid a visit to his village, about 100km from Yaoundé, in his 504 Peugeot. He spent most of the day there. Around 5pm, he took leave. He consulted the petrol gage of the car, found it low and decided to fill the tank with the contents of a jerrycan that was in the trunk of the car. Next to the jerrycan, he found a crumpled wrapping paper. He could not remember having put it in the car trunk. He unwrapped it and found a couple of necklace small chains. His father, who was standing next to him, saw the contents of the paper and said "throw that into the river". He did so, poured the petrol into the tank and drove back to Yaoundé without any further mishap. A few days later, he started suffering from an oedema in the hands and forearms. The medical examinations he underwent and the blood analyses did not suggest any particular diagnosis. This is when I met him in the Faculty corridors.

"Fortunately, my father saw the small chains and told me to discard them, otherwise I would have died of a car accident on my way back to Yaoundé, sais he. And, you see, by now, the feet as well are swollen. I am chained down. This is why you can see me on a bed. I cannot walk any longer. You have seen the *nganga*. Each and every evening, he performs a medication. He immerses my hands and feet into a basin of boiling water in which he has put some herbs to loosen the chains. It is so painful that six strong guys are needed to keep control on me and perform the treatment. Come whenever you wish, you will see that."

John wants me to help him by liaising between the Faculty and him, for his mail, and the papers of the students. He wants me to bring them to him. "You are a white man, he says. You are out of all this business. But do not say anything to the colleagues, and especially not where I am staying." This is how, for a few weeks, I came to drive back and forth between the University campus and the hamlet of the healer.

John is a full professor at the University. He is the owner of several plots in Yaoundé on which he has built housing tenements and a disco-bar. He collects the rents. He lives in a posh villa, owns a Peugeot 504 and a 4x4 vehicle. The sociological literature on Africa[12] has underlined the tensions between the poor villagers on the one hand, and the members of the urban elite put under pressure to redistribute their wealth by a threat of witchcraft that works as an equalizing mechanism. The story of John conforms to this pattern. When visiting the hamlet of the healer, I happen to learn more details. In the village, suspicions soon converge on a poor villager who has a reputation for being envious. He confesses without difficulty having put the small chains in the trunk of the Peugeot car. He is arrested by the gendarmes and put in jail. That particular instance is no longer a case of rumour nor of

---

[12] In that respect, see the synthesis provided by P. Geschiere, *Sorcellerie et politique en Afrique…*, *op. cit.*, p. 164-218.

background media noise. We are facing two identifiable subjects, one who is designated as a witch and admits to it, and the other one who considers himself as his victim. The drama revolves around their own bodies, their discourse, those of their relatives and neighbours, and the material things involved in what happened.

This is what I call a witchcraft crisis of which I have seen only three cases in 45 years. By hearsay, I have had some knowledge of many more, with all the distorting effects that are implied by second hand narratives. Although I might have missed several such events, they are usually spectacular enough not to escape the attention of the entourage of the presumed victim. During all those years, I met neighbours, friends and acquaintances numerous enough to draw my attention on other cases and for me to get the information. But I didn't. Though I heard of very many stories of witchcraft/sorcery I was the first hand witness and personally involved in only three of them. Here, we may be confronted with a problem of definition. I have witnessed many cases of divination (*nikwab* in Mankon language) that broad definitions would include in witchcraft. Here, I only include cases of witchcraft in which there is a victim, a witch, and a number of tangible effects. As an anthropologist intent on watching my entourage, I cannot really say that such paroxystic crises are or were frequent at the time and in places where I lived (NW region and Yaoundé in Cameroon, mostly in the 1970s to 1990s). Misfortunes were frequent. They were not necessarily diagnosed as witchcraft attacks. I seldom saw the batch of symptoms attached to them, although they cannot go unnoticed. Meinrad Hebga[13] also underscores the fact that misfortunes are far from being

---

[13] M. Hebga, "Approche et pratique pastorale", in E. de Rosny (ed.) *Justice et sorcellerie, op. cit.*, p. 325-328.

interpreted in terms of occult attacks. Human errors and health conditions are often taken for what they are and no more, since to validate a suspicion of witchcraft, one needs converging signs and the support of a third party.

For example, my night-watch in Yaoundé lost a 16 years old daughter who died in the bush-taxi in which her father had put her as she was seriously ill, to send her to the village lest she dies in Yaoundé. She died in the taxi while travelling. The entourage did not suspect any occult attack, but only a severe health problem that turned sour – a case of *balok*, as it is said in pidgin (for bad luck), that translates the word *ndon* of the Mbam-Nkam languages, a kind of contamination by misfortune[14] and that does not trigger any overwhelming bout of anxiety, nor any anti-witchcraft cure because it is not caused by a third party.

The ideal type of the witchcraft crisis

P. Geschiere[15] rightly underscores the polymorphism of witchcraft representations, in view of which a case of contamination by a misfortune could be included into witchcraft/sorcery together with anything that belongs with the occult. There are, however, significant differences. Indeed, as regards the crisis (that should be distinguished from the various kinds of discourses although there cannot be any crisis without some sort of verbal validation) one may outline its

---

[14] J.-P. Warnier, *Pre-colonial Mankon: the Development of a Cameroon Chiefdom in its Regional Setting*, Ph.D dissert., Univ. of Pennsylavnia, p. 127-133 and p. 172-176.

[15] P. Geschiere, *Witchcraft, Intimacy and Trust*, op. cit., p. 3-34.

ideal type as follows[16]: 1) the witchcraft crisis starts with a condition that affects the body of the victim, its belongings or its capabilities (that belong with the subject); 2) such a condition can be deciphered in semiotic, and even psychoanalytical terms as illustrated by the psychiatrist and psychoanalyst B. E. Lolo[17]. It is Anye's skin as a bodily envelope of the subject, severely damaged by third degree burns[18], the sensori-motor apparatus of Oyono, incapable to move around in the workshop and to go and practice his trade that structures his existence, or finally the extremities of John's limbs, swollen by the constriction exercised by the chains of occult slavery. The protagonists of the crisis necessarily operate that kind of interpretation; 3) the diagnosis of witchcraft is seldom expressed in the first instance. Being loaded with so much anxiety and threats, it is voiced mostly as a last resort. Under favourable circumstances the subject engages in a therapeutic path in which biomedicine or a pragmatic enquiry on possible mistakes, causes of failure can be found in the first instance; 4) the diagnosis of witchcraft is a dialogic affair. It is formulated by the subject while interacting with his/her entourage, and validated in the end by a healer; 5) throughout the process of elaboration, the anxiety of the actors spreads and accumulates, to reach a climax with the validation, before any cure may start and hopefully alleviate the sufferings of the victim. In the case of Anye', what can be called the period of

---

[16] In order to outline this idéal type, I rely on the three cases I describe in this article and on the many narratives found in the literature, for example in E. de Rosny (ed.), *Justice et sorcellerie, op. cit.,* p. 161, p. 183, etc.

[17] B.E. Lolo, *Mon Afrique. Regardes anthropopsychanalytiques*, Paris, L'Harmattan, 2010.

[18] Concerning the skin, see J.-P. Warnier, *The Pot-King, op. cit.*; M. Salpeteur and J.-P. Warnier "Looking for the Effects of Bodily Organs and Substances through Vernacular Public Autopsy in Cameroon", *Critical African Studies*, vol. 5, n° 3, 2013, p. 153-174.

anxiety-building has been concentrated over a period of only three days. Then, Anye' having died, it did not find any resolution. It contaminated the life of his entourage for a long time. In the case of Oyono and John, this stage spread over several weeks. Its group and dialogic dimensions were particularly obvious in the case of the former since the colleagues of the chief mechanic, that is, some 35 persons, followed the events day after day. The whole group felt the anxiety all the more since the presumed witch could very well be one of the workers, especially those who may have been members of the kin group of the victim. 6) The witchcraft episode calls for a resolution, a tragic one in the case of Anye', a more controlled one in the other two cases; 7) Last but not least, this resolution is achieved with the help of a number of people, that is, in the case of John, his father, who was in attendance right from the start, as a witness to the presence of the small-chains in the trunk of the car and for a follow-up of the events in the village; his wife Joséphine; the members of his household who kept his business running while he was away; the healer and his staff who confirmed the diagnosis, cured John and confounded the culprit; the Gendarmes who put the presumed witch under arrest; the suspect himself who confessed; and the expatriate colleague who liaised, in a neutral way, with the Faculty. This situation is analogous to that of the bereavement circle that builds up around a soldier killed in action[19] and I propose to call it a witchcraft circle - that sort of halo that surrounds a victim of occult attacks. This amounts to quite a few people – so many people that it makes it difficult to restrict the information about the crisis to the secrecy of the small intimate circle. The whole town is informed, talks about

---

[19] S. Audoin-Rouzeau et C. Prochasson, *Sortir de la Grande Guerre: le monde et l'après-1918*, Paris, Tallandier, 2008.

it and transforms the story to its liking. This typology should be useful to introduce relevant distinctions inside the polymorphism underscored by P. Geschiere and to distinguish at least the suspicion from the rumour by hearsay, the accusation, and the actual crisis. Just one example to illustrate this point: cases of contagious mishaps (*ndon* in Mbam-Nkam languages) do not share many common features with an occult attack and does not trigger any equivalent flood of anxiety and group mobilization.

The climactic witchcraft crisis can be easily distinguished from the background noise produced by belief, rumour, gossip, innuendos, the media, on which a large part of the scholarly literature is grounded as it gives precedence to the study of discourse and representations over the ethnography of actual events that can be empirically identified, located and dated. I propose to clearly designate the crisis, to describe it and to distinguish it from its representations[20]. Let me quote an example. In France, in the motorcar era, we live under a permanent threat of a road accident, particularly frequent in town where pedestrians and cyclists are particularly in danger. All categories of accidents once consolidated together, it amounts to some 3500 people killed per year, not taking into consideration twice or three times as many wounded, with their corresponding bereavement circles, to be compared to the 66 million inhabitants of the country, all of them sharing a knowledge and an imaginary concerning this threat and its media coverage. A consultation in the regional daily press and in the tabloids, with assorted photographs, would provide the

---

[20] J. Bonhomme (see note 10 above) underscores the need to distinguish between various elements I amalgamate in a kind of discursive cloud. This is an important critical remark that brings some nuance to my analysis.

sociologist from the planet Mars with a terrifying representation of such a risk. By contrast, does the knowledge we, the inhabitants of our planet, have of the phenomenon alter our daily conducts, except in a marginal way? We are routinely cautious, we look right and left before crossing a street, we fasten our seat belts. If we ride a bicycle, we may protect our head with a helmet – a "*blindage*" of sorts[21]. Are our professional, family, leisure activities – dependent as they are on the car and our walking in the public space – emptied of any pragmatic dimension? Do they lose their own logic and density? They are serious activities, as it were, that can be submitted to sociological or economic enquiries in which the threat of accidents, and our knowledge of that topic, would be most of the time absent or pushed to the margins. Why should Africa enjoy such a dubious privilege of being a land of witchcraft to such an extent that it would pervade all the activities of its subjects whereas, de facto, witchcraft crises only affect a minority and does not overturn the pragmatic routines of everyday life? In order to complement and to qualify this picture, it should be advisable to document all the possible patterns between rumours, innuendos and the empirically observed crisis.

For a sociology of the witchcraft crisis

One has to clearly distinguish between the event of the witchcraft crisis and the background noise of rumour and belief. To achieve this, we need a sociology or, as it were, an epidemiology of such paroxystic events. We need figures,

---

[21] "Blindage" (armour or armouring) is a terms widely used in francophone Africa to designate any ritual action meant to increase the résistance of a subject to occult attacks.

18

frequencies, prevalence indicators. In my opinion, the empirically detectable occurrences are few and far between. May I say again that in 45 years, I have been a first-hand witness of only three of them (which does not mean that there were not many more in my surroundings but that I didn't come across them). M. Salpeteur[22] who did research on vernacular autopsies in Western Cameroon, has registered only 11 diagnoses of witchcraft attacks out of 100 autopsies, the other diagnoses referring to various causes or to health conditions to be addressed by forensic medicine, that is, a figure significantly inferior to 11% of all death cases since a vernacular post mortem is performed only in case there is a doubt – a rather rare occurrence.

One may object that, regarding such a phenomenon, a quantitative enquiry meant to construct indicators is not feasible. Yet several scholars have tried their hands at it. Not without results. C. Fisiy[23] has documented the practice of witchcraft trials in Cameroonian high courts. R. Nantchouang published a rejoinder, with charts and figures[24]. We know (see the case of John) that, in cases of a witchcraft crisis ending in an accusation, the suspect or suspects are likely to be put on arrest by the police of gendarmes, detained and tried, which produces police reports and judiciary archives. A criminologist could perhaps produce indicators in a given administrative district (in Cameroon, from one Region to the next, scholars

---

[22] M. Salpeteur, *Du palais à l'autopsie. Les doublures animales dans une chefferie bamiléké (Cameroun)*, Thèse de doctorat en anthropologie, Paris, Muséum national d'histoire naturelle, 2009.

[23] C. Fisiy, "Containing Occult Practices: Witchcraft Trials in Cameron", *African Studies Review*, vol. 41, n° 3, 1998, p. 143-163.

[24] R. Nantchouang, "Economie: sorcellerie et externalités économiques", in E. de Rosny (ed.), *Justice et sorcellerie, op. cit.*, p. 139-140.

mention considerable differences in their frequencies) and to assess the reliability of such sources – admittedly low.

It would be conceivable to cross-compare such data with other indicators, however rough they may be. In Cameroon, in case of health problems, people first address the biomedical facilities – dispensary, hospital, general practitioner. If there is no improvement in their condition, they may address other facilities where they can find alternative cures – with traditional doctors (*nganga*), in prosperity churches of various denominations, including the Pentecostal ones that practice exorcism. With a modicum of patience, the number of consultations per month in hospital practice, in Yaoundé or in lesser cities, should be accessible, as would be the number of consultations with traditional doctors concerning suspected cases of witchcraft. In my knowledge of urban and rural environments in Yaoundé and the NW Region is to be trusted, their number is comparatively small as compared to the number of medical personnel engaged in biomedical care. By contrast, this does not seem to be the case in SAR if the Ralushai Report quoted by P. Geschiere[25] is to be trusted. However, it is not easy to find the reasons of such a contrast: the lack of medical facilities, the poverty of large sectors of the population, especially in townships, or other causes. It should also be said that the number of practitioners is but a weak indicator as against the number of consultations.

---

[25] Commission of Inquiry into Witchcraft Violence and Ritual Murders, *Report of the Commission of Inquiry into Witchcraft Violence and Ritual Murders in the Northern Province of the Republic of South Africa (Ralushai Commission)*, Northern Province, Minister of Safety and Security, 1996; quoted by P. Geschiere, "The State, Witchcraft and the Limits of the Law: Cameroon and South Africa", in E. de Rosny (ed.), *Justice et sorcellerie, op. cit.*, p. 106.

Things situation may have changed since 2000. The same P. Geschiere[26] is of the opinion that the witchcraft complex has increased and developed, although it is impossible to provide any proof of such a statement. I would hypothesize that witchcraft discourses take more and more space in gossips, rumours and the media, if only because of the spectacular increase of wealth inequalities, of poverty, of the proliferation of Pentecostal churches the stock in trade of which is constituted by the fear of witchcraft attacks, and also because of the liberalization of the daily press in many an African country since the rise of democratic unrest in the 1990s, that has triggered the proliferation of newspaper titles and has given an opportunity to publish articles on many different topics, provided they were sensational and didn't touch upon established leaders or the political regime. Accordingly, this is how Julien Bonhomme[27] has conducted a detailed research on witchcraft rumours in Gabon, and, more recently, in Senegal, that, quite obviously, concerns the media and their communication strategies (this is already very enlightening) but does not provide any information on the prevalence of actual crises in the population.

Moreover, researches on such topics in Africa often suffer from a methodological bias. By construction, some occupations – psychiatrists, psychoanalysts, pastors, traditional doctors, ethnographers doing research by making use of the verbal statements of their informants, are more exposed to this type of discourse. If their endeavour gives them a privileged access to a qualitative perception of such phenomena, it precludes a quantitative grasp – however vague – of the

---

[26] P. Geschiere, *Witchcraft, Intimacy and Trust, op. cit.,* p. 182.
[27] J. Bonhomme, *Les voleurs de sexe…, op. cit.;* "La sorcellerie à l'heure des medias", art cité.

frequency of crises and of their impact on the pragmatic life of ordinary subjects. Among ethnologists, those who do not stay at length in the field and want to study witchcraft are particularly exposed to this methodological difficulty resulting from such an ethnographic situation, more or less immersed in a given environment or disembedded from it. By contrast, economists doing research in Africa seldom meet with such cases. Thus E. Kamdem[28], a sociologist of corporate business, who is the Director of the School of social and economic sciences (ESSEC) in Douala, clearly stated during the Conference "Justice and Witchcraft": "the origin of success in business is to be found in professional qualification, personal gifts and ambition", that is, not in occult practices. We find similar views with anthropologists like Jane Guyer who conduct research on economic activities in Africa. I will return to this question later on.

Such a bias combines with a second one that comes from the social categories with which scholars conduct their research. As far as the four strategic categories identified by E. Galland are concerned (the staff at Parliament, young women, "big men" and urban youth) the result may be significantly different from what could be inferred from an enquiry with mechanics, lorry drivers, building contractors or carpenters – that is, with social categories whose activity produces more tangible, more material and easily objectifiable results than those of white collar workers or of relatively inactive categories (young women or urban youth) who, from a subjective point of view, it seems to me, are more likely to yield to the discourse on the occult concerning the requisites of social success. In all such cases, the anthropological discourse is a second hand one

---

28 E. Kamdem, "Sorcellerie, organisation et comportement dans l'entreprise", in E. de Rosny (ed), *Justice et sorcellerie, op. cit.*, p. 197 and 199.

and not the narrative of actual crises that may be found in all social categories (including mechanics) as can be seen in the case of Oyono described above. Enquiring in twelve Cameroonian business firms with Cameroonian capital, leadership and employees in 1992 together with Alain Henry and Emmanuel Kamdem, I never heard any suggestion re. occult practices. Neither did my two colleagues.

Lastly - third difficulty – by contrast, any enquiry based on interviews gives a privileged access to discursive expression, to what can be said in so many words. The researcher must assess most critically the data in order to vet the narratives and sort out different types of discourses depending on the contents and the speech situation, giving access to different types of lived experiences, some of them pertaining to actual crises in which the subjects have been involved, with given events that can be dated and documented or with given practices lending themselves to ethnographic descriptions, as against discourses belonging with the imaginary of witchcraft and its retinue of rumours.

What is at stake?

What is the relevance of these comments concerning a sociological endeavour? If, in Africa, the family, work, professional activities, consumption, daily life are always and everywhere provided with a kind of witchcraft or occult lining from the point of view of the subjects, how is it possible to build up a sociology grounded in empirical research, the object of which consists in tangible practice? Even, and above all when it comes to the political organization, with its balance of power, alliances, networks, co-optation, finances? If it were to be lined up with occult forces throughout, it would lose any substance of its own. It would be like a shadow-theatre in which the only relevant component would be the occult lining of things, that any empirical study would fail to attain. It would disqualify any historical sociology of politics based on empirical enquiries concerning actual practice. The only thing it could achieve would be to get in line with the discourse of the media. I feel all the more free to write such a statement that, in the past, I have yielded to the bias of giving precedence to the narratives without making them clearly distinct from the events behind them[29].

I am convinced that imaginaries and representations deserve full-fledged research on their own rights, but at the same time, it seems important to me to get rid of anything approaching a Magritte effect by drawing a clear distinction between the real economy, power relationships, social dynamics on the one hand, and the various kinds of verbal constructions on the other hand. For example, Janet MacGaffey has analysed the real economy of ex-Zaire (now DRC)[30] and Jane Guyer, on her side, has considered the provision systems in foodstuffs or currency or several African towns[31]. In none of their many publications is witchcraft ever mentioned, not even by the side. It does not turn up in the index of any of their books. Such activities belong with, as it were, serous practice, devoid of any occult lining, including in

---

[29] M. Rowlands and J.-P. Warnier, "Sorcery, Power and the Modern State in Cameroon", *Man*, vol. 23, n° 1, 1988, p. 118-132.

[30] J. MacGaffey, *The Real Economy of Zaire. The Contribution of Smuggling and Other Unofficial Activities to ational Wealth*, London: James Currey, 1991.

[31] J.I. Guyer (ed.), *Feeding African Cities: Essays in Regional Social History*, London: Manchester University Press/IAI, 1987; *Money Matters: Instability, Values and Social Payments in the Modern History of West African Communities*, Portsmouth, Heineman, 1995; J.I. Guyer, *Margnial Gains. Monetary Transactions in Atlantic Africa*, Chicago: The University of Chicago Press, 1997.

the perception of the subjects themselves, unless they are prompted by leading questions. Such a silence should question all the analysts of witchcraft in Africa. How comes that Jane Guyer does not find even a hint at occult practices whereas others, doing research on them, find their footprints at the heart of economic imaginaries? This question amounts to a test and deserves an answer. The case of power relationships is more complex since they are prone to drape themselves in the discourse of occult forces. But even in that case, the efficacy of power relationships rests in alliances, exclusions, co-operation, bargaining in which the threat of occult attacks, or rather vague hints in that direction are part of the political power game, yet no more than the threat of physical violence or the illegitimate use of money. Most political scientists in Africa take representations and imaginaries into account, yet at their proper place – without claiming that they load the political dices in any systematic way. Accordingly, I will re-word my questioning in the following way: when collapsing together various levels of discourse and actual practice, don't Africanist scholars lock themselves up into a circular methodology and epistemology that precludes their access to the pragmatics and seriousness of at least some of their objects?

It seems to me that African studies suffer from a cognitive gap. When reading studies in witchcraft, the latter seems to inhere all the actions of the subjects. When reading the publications of economists, some political scientists and sociologists like Jane Guyer and Emmanuel Kamdem, the activities performed in the very same African societies are seen as pragmatic, serious, devoid of any occult lining, and amenable to enquiries and analyses with the usual tools of the social sciences. It seems important to paste together those two pieces of social life and to measure the cognitive gap that separates them. Gregory Bateson[32] was one of the first anthropologists to perceive this type of phenomenon and to put it at the core of his studies in schismogenesis likely to affect individuals, groups, families and organizations.

As Urmila Mohan and myself have suggested elsewhere[33], it may very well be that such a cognitive gap is part and parcel of the compliance with the discourse of occult forces, because it prompts the subject to reduce it by stepping into an imaginary, that is, according to the famous expression of Deleuze, a domain of indeterminacy between what is real and what is not. However, if such is the case, and if, as I think following P. Geschiere, it is counter-productive to feed such belief systems, as Pentecostal churches and Cameroonian high courts do or have done, then, if only for ethical reasons, but also for scientific ones, isn't it advisable to shun anything that would look like a Magritte effect and to be more critical and sober in the many publications in social sciences on witchcraft in Africa?

What could a fair sociological program, designed to analyse such a phenomenon, look like? First of all, it would have to collect all the relevant information from rumours, suspicions, gossips, bar conversations, ethnographic interviews bearing on belief and media production, to fit them into a hierarchy and to vet them through the usual tools of media studies and content analysis. Next, it would have to conduct a sociology of practice, including discursive ones, while carrying on the all too rare ethnographic descriptions of actual crises as I have

---

[32] G. Bateson, *Steps to an Ecology of Mind*, New York: Ballantines Books, 1972.

[33] U. Mohan and J.-P. Warnier, "Marching the Devotional Subject: the Bodily and Material Cultures of Religion", *Journal of Material Culture*, Vol 22 (4), p. 369-384, 2017.

sketched their profile. It would also pursue the attempts by C. Fisiy, R. Nantchouang, M. Salpeteur, to collect figures and indicators. It could also extent data acquisition to similar practices – alternative or competing ones – as a means of control or comparison: the number of consultations in biomedicine, with traditional doctors, attendance at healing churches, region by region, as has been done by the Ralushai report in SAR[34]. This being done, one would have to bring back again, within the sociological analysis, everything that had been left between brackets at the point of departure in order to gage the inflation (or deflation) of witchcraft representations against the ethnography of crises and the patterns of objectifiable data concerning actual events and practice. It should be possible to assess possible discrepancies between the two sets of data. For good measure, one could compare popular or educated narratives on witchcraft with the enquiries conducted by economists or anthropologists like J. Guyer on pragmatic activities like transport, provision systems, trade, building, etc. as it were from the outside of the discourse on/by witchcraft, conspicuously devoid of any suspicion of occult practice. Lastly, it should be possible to document any possible cognitive gap between the frequency of witchcraft crises and the large space witchcraft is occupying in the media, in evangelical preaching, and… in the social sciences. In brief, the aim would be to deconstruct any possible Magritte effect. Is it far too ambitious? Certainly it is. But isn't it the price to be paid for sound scholarly knowledge and professional ethics?

---

[34] Commission of Inquiry into Witchcraft Violence and Ritual Murders. *Report of the Commission of Inquiry into Witchcraft, op. cit.*

PART II

2

Witchcraft and Discourse Genres:
From Intimate Stories to Public Rumours

Julien Bonhomme
École Normale Supérieure,
Laboratoire d'Anthropologie Sociale, Paris

We cannot thank Jean-Pierre Warnier enough for his poignant critique of the inflation in the amount of works done on witchcraft. I agree with him on the fact that Africanists (including myself) focus a lot and maybe even too much on the subject. There is a risk that this becomes sort of questionable line of business at some point, with the anthropologist looking increasingly more of a popular press journalist hungry for sensationalism or a Pentecostal preacher whose denunciation of sorcerers and other demons serves to justify his ministry of healing. That being said, for debate's sake, I shall play the role of the devil-sorcerer's advocate by putting forward some thoughts inspired by Warnier.

In *Régner au Cameroun*, a previous piece by Warnier, the denunciation of the Magritte effect struck the right chord in highlighting the distinction between practices and representations on the subject of power[1]. It seems to me, however, that the argument is less relevant as regards witchcraft. Warnier compares the "representation of witchcraft" (that he takes to include discourse, rumour, gossip

---

[1] J.-P. Warnier, *Régner au Cameroun. Le Roi-Pot*, Paris, Karthala, 2009. *The Pot-King, the Body and Technologies of Power*, Leiden: Brill, 2007.

and belief) with witchcraft itself, which manifests in the form of "crises" that affect the body and translate into conducts (therapeutic itineraries laden with rituals). But these crises are also matter of discourse specifically: suspicions cast by someone close to the victim; gossip going around in the neighbourhood; diagnoses made by a diviner or a pastor. A witch crisis is based on a myriad of stories that are as many partial accounts of the affair (because one is always a witch in the eyes of another). It is also worth noting that for the three crises that he reported, Warnier did not have access to observable practices himself, but relied on reports by third parties: the parents and colleagues of Anye and Oyono, who gave him an interpretation of their misfortunes in terms of witchcraft. Rather than a distinction between reality and its representation, I propose then to analyse witchcraft in terms of different discourse genres (without denying the importance of body and ritual).

Firstly, common representations. These are generic discourses that are often artificial, typically put out by interlocutors in response to our questions about sorcerers and witchcraft. At the beginning of an investigation, this type of discourse allows for a general idea of the phenomenon. However, to avoid the pitfall of intellectualist approaches (whose ontological or cosmological variants are the latest manifestations), we should be careful not to systematise these common representations and turn them into "indigenous theories".

Secondly, public stories. These are edifying stories that are spread all the more easily as they involve third parties but not directly the persons who peddle them or their relatives. "The radio announced that a man was robbed of his genitalia yesterday by shaking hands with a stranger". "A politician who died at election time had been cursed by a rival". Beyond the word-of-mouth, the media play a leading role in the proliferation of these stories. There is also a cause-and-effect relationship between the rise of the popular press following the liberalisation of the media sector in the 1990s in many African countries and the proliferation of this kind of discourse: witchcraft has moved into the media age. To spread these stories enables the public to share outrage, to play with fears, or, simply to be entertained by a good story. The public's attitude towards them can be more distanced – at times amused or in disbelief – since not personally involved. It is therefore impossible to study occult stories spread by the media without at the same time focusing on the production of journalistic information and its reception[2].

Thirdly, private and intimate stories. These are the ones that directly involve our informants or their relatives (this corresponds, in Warnier's terms, to "crises"). People do not often speak of these, at least not to strangers. Only the closest will be in on this secret and will find themselves involved in therein too (as Jeanne Favret-Saada has shown about French peasant witchcraft[3]). Contrary to public stories that are easy to collect, private stories are accessible only to an ethnographer close enough to the protagonists so that they will confide in him (or her) their misfortunes, at the cost, however, of finding himself or herself involved in the matter (which shows in the case of Jean, who opens himself up to Warnier through his wife so as to ask for his help while also asking him not to speak of it to his colleagues). This criterion of ethnographic proximity

[2] J. Bonhomme, "La sorcellerie à l'ère des medias", *in* S. Fancello (dir.), *Penser la sorcellerie en Afrique*, Paris, Hermann, 2015, p. 83-116.

[3] J. Favret-Saada, *Deadly Words: Witchcraft in Bocage*, London, Cambridge University Press, 1980.

seems to me more pertinent than the distinction, among ethnographic methods, between observation (access to practices) and interview (access to discourse) that Warnier relates to the distinction between witchcraft and its representation. Intimate stories still relate to discourse, even if they belong to a different genre from that of public rumour. We should however keep from radically contrasting public and private stories. A private story can be elevated to the dimension of a public one when the media seizes it. Conversely, any public story hides a private one that could be studied ethnographically by collecting the protagonists' testimonies.

Despite these distinctions, there is no reason to assume that intimate stories alone would constitute real witchcraft, against which public stories would then be false manifestations thereof, and therefore, not meaningful ones. The latter are part and parcel of this protean phenomenon that is witchcraft. This means that they ought to be understood in their own terms: one must study how they circulate, how they are told, and how the public relates to them, in contrast to intimate stories. I hope that, by bringing to the fore rumours about sex thieves, killer mobile phone numbers and deadly alms[4], I have helped prove the interest that there could be in studying these kinds of stories. They shed new light on some of the dynamics of contemporary African societies, whether in relation to urban sociality, cosmopolitanism, xenophobia, gender relations, the appropriation of communication technologies, or violence and the so-called popular justice.

---

[4] J. Bonhomme, *The Sex Thieves. The Anthropology of a Rumor*, Chicago: HAU Books, 2016; J. Bonhomme, "Les numéros de téléphone portable qui tuent. Épidémiologie culturelle d'une rumeur transnationale", *Tracés*, n° 21, 2011, p. 125-150; J. Bonhomme and J. Bondaz, *L'offrande de la mort. Une rumeur au Sénégal*, Paris, CNRS éditions, 2017.

According to Warnier, paying too much attention to the discourses on witchcraft would imply neglect of its practices and the empirical observation thereof. The critique may not always hold true, even if it is necessary to recognise the weakness in certain works dedicated to social imaginaries, which ignore the "pragmatic seriousness" in and of ordinary activities. For example, when Émilie Guitard reports on rumours of witchcraft associated with garbage in Northern Cameroon[5], it is an original way of addressing more concrete issues. What must be done of nail clippings and menstrual waste? How must we handle the garbage that invades the public space? To talk about witchcraft is not to speculate on a metaphysical otherworld; it is a way to study more prosaic realities. Far from being confined along the lines of representation, rumours of witchcraft may rest, as do private stories, on "identified, dated and circumstantial events", and therefore, allow for the observation of sensori-motor conducts involving bodies and affects. Many of these are not limited to the propagation of abstract and fleeting narratives but have concrete repercussions, for example, when one man, out of fear, publicly accuses another of having robbed him of his genitalia after shaking his hand, causing the latter to be lynched by an angry mob. By reifying the distinction between reality and its representation, between words and things, we risk neglecting both the discursive dimension of crises (intimate stories) and the concrete manifestation of rumours (public incidents).

Another idea in Warnier's piece, which I think deserves to be commented on, is that of the rarity of witchcraft. It is true

---

[5] E. Guitard, "Between Municipal Management and Sorcery Uses of Waste. Cameroonian Institutions Faced with 'Sorcerers Covered with Refuse' (Garoua and Maroua)", *Cahiers d'études africaines*, n°231-232, 2018.

that events pertaining to this are rare occurrence and it is glad that it is so! Thenceforth, whether it is sporadic accusations of penis snatching or Jean's misfortunes as narrated by Warnier, we are really dealing with crises, that is to say, with events that disturb the fabric of everyday life. Likewise, if it is common to bring up the latest occult rumours in ordinary conversations, it is to a much lesser extent than people discuss the price of rice at the market, electricity cuts or the next elections. It is important to be reminded of this so as to avoid thinking that people are obsessed with witchcraft to the point of seeming slightly paranoid. Warnier's proposal to develop indicators to measure this rarity is welcome, even if it would be complicated to implement. The police and judicial archives seem lacking to me, for example, because only a small fraction of the witchcraft affairs reach the police station or the court.

If witchcraft crises remain rare, I nevertheless feel that Warnier underestimates their prevalence by mentioning only three cases in forty-five years of field work. My own field work conducted between 2000 and 2008 in Gabon with urban and rural *nganga* brought me to a different conclusion. The prolonged immersion among these witchdoctors allowed me to be the direct witness of dozens of crises like those of Anye, Oyono and Jean. I collected the intimate stories of the "victims" whose misfortunes were most often associated with family troubles and to the hatred that broods within them. I took part in the rituals destined to deliver them from their affliction by soothing their troubles and by purifying their bodies (Warnier is therefore right, witchcraft is a matter of body and affects)[6]. But it would be expected to hear much about the occult when working with the *nganga*. Their

---

[6] J. Bonhomme, *Le miroir et le crâne. Parcours initiatique du Bwete Misoko (Gabon)*, Paris, CNRS éditions/Éditions de la MSH, 2006.

divinatory sessions represent a scene where any minor trouble can be turned into witchcraft. If I had instead conducted fieldwork in medical clinics, I would have come across more ordinary patients rather than victims of witchcraft. In witchcraft, as it is the case more often than not, it is all a matter of ethnographic point of view. But beyond the biases of investigation, could there not be other distinctions between Cameroon and Gabon, to explain this divergence of conclusions? Or between the 1970s and 2000s? Drawing on his own field work experience, Peter Geschiere notes that witchcraft has now become an ordinary subject of discussion whilst people were reluctant to talk about it in the first decades after independence[7].

Let us add a comparative dimension to these considerations: it has been a few years since I left Gabon for Senegal (Dakar, and to a lesser extent, the Serer region). There, I was not much confronted with intimate stories on witchcraft even if occult rumours circulate profusely in the local press. From the 1960s onwards, the Ortigues evoked a decline of witchcraft in urban areas, stating that it was at the cost of increased "maraboutage" (evil magic): fewer witches (*dëmm* in Wolof), but more sorcery (*liggéey*)[8]. That being said, the observation about the unequal prevalence of witchcraft in Gabon and in Senegal comes, likely, from different ethnographic points of view. In Senegal, I did not conduct extensive fieldwork among the "marabouts" (the local equivalent of Gabonese nganga), even though I was led to meet several of them during my investigation on Senegalese

---

[7] P. Geschiere, *Witchcraft, Intimacy and Trust: Africa in Comparison*, Chicago, University of Chicago Press, 2013, p. 182.

[8] M.-C. Ortigues and E. Ortigues, *OEdipe africain*, Paris, L'Harmattan, 1984 [1966], p. 195.

wrestling. Beside their physical training, wrestlers devote a significant part of their time and resources to "mystical preparation". For this purpose, they consult marabouts, sometimes several dozens. But wrestling magic is rarely associated with witchcraft as it is deemed a legitimate practice: wrestlers have the right to use their resources as they see fit so as to win. As an integral part of the wrestling show, the mystical dimension of combat is carefully staged during the preliminary rituals performed within the arena.[9]

That being said, I was unintentionally witness to two witchcraft crises that occurred in my neighbourhood in Senegal. In the first case, Falou, a strong body-builder, fell ill all of a sudden and was on bed rest for months without medical examinations being able to fix the cause of his illness. According to him, he was a victim of witchcraft as a result of a family dispute over inheritance. To be cured, he went to see various witchdoctors in Dakar and in "the village". In the second case, Assane, young and ambitious entrepreneur, found himself paralysed from the bottom half of the body for an entire day, as a result, he said, of mystical attacks by jealous competitors. Since then, prior to each of his important business dealings, he "shields" himself. From my point of view (which is ethnographically situated), if witchcraft crises are uncommon, they are not so rare as to be almost non-existent.

The debate certainly deserves to be pursued. But we can already be grateful toward Jean-Pierre Warnier for helping us put witchcraft back to its rightful place in social life, to remain conscious of ethnographic biases when we want to measure its prevalence, and to distinguish more clearly the regimes of

---

[9] J. Bonhomme and L. Gabail, "Lutte mystique. Sport, magie et sorcellerie au Sénégal", *Cahiers d'études africaines*, à paraître.

discourse that it presupposes and the types of empirical observation to which it can give rise.

3

For a Hermeneutics of Witchcraft

Patrice Yengo

Université Marien Ngouabi-Brazzaville,
Imaf (Institut des mondes africains), EHESS-Paris

> "Once we have let evil in,
> It no longer requires that we believe in it."
> — Frantz Kafka, *Journal Intime*, 1948

It is a difficult exercise that which Jean-Pierre Warnier invites us toward. I could have avoided it by pretending to my aversion for the term "witchcraft", which, as I recently expressed it, is far too polysemous to be basis for epistemology[1]. But this kind of attitude would only stem from bad faith and would ignore the truth of the matter at hand. Still, to delve into the critique of a text to which we generally agree, without diminishing it, is a challenge, especially when it comes with specific tasks that cannot be avoided. Except to exacerbate its asperities, to "complicate" its object, as per Claude Lefort's formula re communism[2], that is to say, to be extricated from the hold of situations and their spontaneous interpretation, to ground these within their complex determinations and the context of their enunciation. Still, without losing in sight the fact that these determinations are part of the global phenomenon of the symbolical constitution

---

[1] P. Yengo, *Les mutations sorcières dans le bassin du Congo. Du ventre et de sa politique*, Paris, Karthala, 2016.

[2] C. Lefort, *La complication. Retour sur le communisme*, Paris, Fayard, 1999.

of the social world. This is the picture that Jean-Pierre Warnier paints in broad strokes, pleading for an "epidemiology" of the witchcraft crisis defined as "paroxysmal episode during which a subject, clearly identified, acquires certainty, confirmed by those around, to be victim of a witchcraft attack[3]."

What is allowed by way of such "epidemiological" approach, which implies at once the subject, victim in his body and belongings, and the surroundings, in the validation of the diagnosis, but also requires recourse to external third parties as source (presumed responsible for the attack) and as solution (therapist)? What does it teach us? If not the need to understand the lived experience of witchcraft from the inside and to build from this certainty "a set of knowledge and techniques to allow the signs to speak for themselves and so as to uncover their meaning"[4]. This approach, deemed hermeneutic, is, I think, that in which Jean-Pierre Warnier's text engages us. But to get there, we should perhaps overcome some pitfalls.

The first is that pertaining to belief and certainty. I still have in mind the statements of Professor Mamadou Koumaré, one of my seniors in Pharmacology, at a symposium on traditional medicine in Bamako, who said that he learned from traditional healers that the matter of witchcraft would have to be considered only if the patient brought it up themselves. This leads us to make the distinction between belief and certainty. Because, in my opinion, witchcraft is more a matter of certainty than belief.

Belief presupposes the possibility of doubt. Certainty is about what is probable but bears no doubt, and is installed

---

[3] J.-P. Warnier, "Ceci n'est pas un sorcier. De l'effet Magritte en sorcellerie", *Politique africaine*, n° 146, 2017, p. 127.

[4] M. Foucault, Words and things, Paris, Gallimard, 1966

along a working grid that is constantly re-adjusted to encompass new ideas. Chance, this "faceless god", as Paul Valéry called it, ceases to be efficient. There cannot be any contingency either as disappears the fortuitous character that can cover an event, which results in a relentless causal concatenation behind which is inexorably looming intentional hand, often human, and evil. The reason for which certainty is always redundant: "absolute certainty", it is said. We are far from the absoluteness that is presupposed here, or the allusive character to which it refers. As to think that it is from this absoluteness that comes the force of truth, which excludes doubt and in which is its referential function: absolute certainty. What can a person be certain of, but himself? Certainty creates conviction, thus becoming self-referential.

Belief does not exclude the fact that what is believed is illusion, on the contrary. Indeed, that this contravenes conventional logic, rationality, that it makes no sense or that it is simply absurd does not undermine the belief itself. Proof that belief holds, beyond doubt, openness to the absurd, that is, the possibility to assume a world incapable of giving meaning to life: Tertullian c*redo quia absurdum*. Certainty does not brush against the absurd; it relies on evidence, that is to say, in the etymological sense, on what is simply seen, precisely, immediately. And certainty allows itself to be apprehended so clearly and distinctly that the mind cannot be doubtful of it. Witchcraft is, in this perspective, based on primary evidence, in the manner that it is delivered in the order of discourse by the formulations of desire or intentionality. A memory of my adolescence comes to mind.

In the *fulla-fulla* (mini-bus) that takes me back on this rainy day from the station of Pointe-Noire, we repetitively come across this nun who is completely drenched on her motorcycle.

She overtakes us at each stop until we catch up with her in turn. The game lasts for a while until the driver, tongue-in-cheek, embarks on a sort of indictment against "all those people who come to deceive us with their religion." Brawl and laughter that the driver excites even more with statements that are increasingly more anti-religious: "Trust me! The day that I have the means to crush them one by one, I won't stop myself." One passenger's reply: "Start with this one." The driver's response: "If the opportunity arose, do you think that I won't?"

A little later, as we had moved on to something completely different, we reach the Kassaï roundabout. Taking the turn too fast at the roundabout and seeking to avoid a truck on the left, the *fulla-fulla* abruptly veers onto the right and, despite braking hard, cannot avoid the nun, who is violently thrown onto the pavement. Consternation and silence takes over on board. The police, present on scene, immediately intervene whilst we evacuate the mini-bus. Bleeding and unconscious, the nun is taken to the Adolphe Sice hospital, which is not far away. What strikes me at that moment, is the driver's stupefaction and aphasia, incapable to respond the police's questions but repeating, incessantly: "No, I did not do that!" Those who, some time ago, laughed at his irreverent remarks, now accuse him of having his wish come true. Quasi unanimous form of retribution that he is spared from only in the repetition of his mantra. Struck that his remarks have surpassed expectations, he wonders, at that moment if he is the "owner" of that thing that made his wish come true. This is the strongest memory that I have of this accident. We were a handful to want to answer the police's questions, but our voices were lost in the general uncertainty: is it not him who declared wanting to run her over?

From this example we can take that certainty is consistent as it offers guarantees that we expect. In this particular case, the guarantee of conformity to what is expected implies the wish that carries and realises the omen. Yet, even prior to its performative intentionality, the evidence, as it reveals itself here, cannot be established as criteria for truth. Because it is blinding. It imposes onto us an optical sense that has more to do with a feeling than a sort of rational intuition, and even a shamanic clairvoyance. Hence the need to distance ourselves from it because at a certain level of exigency, there is no truth that is so obvious.

To remove witchcraft from the influence of rumour, of gossip, J.-P. Warnier recommends its analysis as phenomenon at its paroxysmal moment: the witchcraft crisis. As phenomenon and not only evidence. Which indicates that if witchcraft implies certainty, not belief, what opens here is a hermeneutics. Because "perfect evidence and its correlative, truth, present themselves as an idea inherent in the desire to know, to fulfil the significant intention.[5] A hermeneutics of the fact of witchcraft is not irrational. It allows for the observation of witchcraft as neither an arbitrary narrative nor an impossible story, and in its quality of certainty, a witchcraft crisis is then the moment at which witchcraft allows itself to be caught in its dynamics of concealment that is as bright as it is revealing.

A second pitfall relates to the question of evil, which is brought up by Rosny in response to Alban Bensa at the symposium in Yaoundé that Jean-Pierre Warner mentions in his text[6]. It is undeniable that today's Pentecostal sways

---

[5] E. Husserl, *Méditations cartésiennes. Introduction à la phénoménologie*, Paris, J. Vrin, coll. "Biblio-thèque des textes philosophiques", 1986, p. 10.

[6] J.-P. Warnier, "Ceci n'est pas un sorcier…", art. cité, p. 125. Voici exactement ce que dit Éric de Rosny: "Dire qu'elle [la sorcellerie] n'existe pas, c'est nier tout simplement avec une certaine naïveté l'existence d'une

develop at the forefront of witchcraft defined as evil, but let us not forget that witchcraft has always legitimised evangelistic campaigns in the Congo basin since the 15th century, with, at its peak, a crusade against fetishes, statues and other figures of worship assumed idolatry. As if fetish had to do with statues only. In Jean-Pierre Warnier's text, the "two or three chains" that John finds in his car show this clearly: any object, as banal as it may seem, can serve as fetish when it is charged[7] by a *nganga*. Let us admit that in thinking of it as evil, religions of salvation have managed to give to witchcraft its metaphysical depth but, insofar as metaphysics tends to be a theodicy in the religious mysteries, they make it lose its social efficiency by assimilating the devil, Satan. The scandal of this assimilation comes in the fact of the proliferation of child sorcerers in the streets of Kinshasa. Exorcised and "born again", witchcraft still marks them negatively and they are rejected to the streets.

In reality, religion speaks of sin and the fall of Man that it associates to suffering in the expiatory destiny of humanity, where the negativity that comes with witchcraft speaks to the individual's connection to the world, the human with his self, and more precisely, the disconnection of the subject to his

---

certaine perversité dans ce monde [...]. Ce besoin pervers de nuire qui gît au coeur de l'homme n'est ni accessible ni même concevable autrement que dans un système de représentation socioculturelle. Si vous dites que la sorcellerie n'existe pas, c'est que vous vivez les effets du mal selon un autre paradigme [...]. Car les racines du Mal demeurent un mystère en leur fond et chaque société a dû s'en protéger à sa manière et pour ce faire, se donner ou adhérer à une vision de la vie". É. de Rosny (dir.), *Justice et sorcellerie. Colloque international de Yaoundé, 17-19 mars 2005*, Paris, Karthala, 2006, p. 28-29. On peut se rapporter aussi à la critique que je fais des travaux de ce colloque: P. Yengo, "Rosny, É. de (dir.). – *Justice et sorcellerie. Colloque international de Yaoundé, 17-19 mars 2005*", *Cahiers d'études africaines*, n° 189-190, 2008, p. 372-378.

[7] Des chaînettes chargées d'enserrer les pieds du conducteur, la charge ici est toute de puissance analogique.

environment. It is clear that witchcraft poses an ontological problem. However, the discourse that we can hold of it must not seek to define its in-self but to uncover the certainty that begs it. If the epidemiology of the witchcraft crisis is the gateway to this certainty, it should be noted that the latter does not speak directly to it, and it does not objectify it either, but finds it already interpreted, from both the social and private points of view, in relevant terms that combine belief, customs and tradition. All of which push for T.K.M. Buakasa – whose work we could not recommend enough – to say that witchcraft "is an ideological discourse that speaks for a different reality"[8] expressed in the fact thereof and operating within it. It is in this manner that we can manage to put words to concrete situations and to approach in speculative terms, existential thoughts and their tautological symbols, and that we can tackle this complex social truth that forms within the witchcraft crisis, bringing to light the existential dimension by which is realised the original possession of the social truth even if this is only implicitly.

A hermeneutics of witchcraft is a reflection at the heart of the individual's experience, fuelled by pre-existing knowledge and marked by its existential dimension. Proceeding from experience and rapport to the world, it is not only determined through witchcraft when at its crisis peak, but deepens it to reveal the obscure, contradictory, neglected and concealed aspects of this rapport. The witchcraft crisis illuminates, from its own meaningfulness, that reality which becomes positive from its own negativity. For evil, which it is the expression of, does not imply the disappearance of good or the transgression

---

[8] T. K. M. Buakasa, *L'impensé du discours? Kindoki et Nkisi en pays Kongo du Zaïre*, Kinshasa/Bruxelles, Presses universitaires du Zaïre/Unaza-Cedaf, 1973, p. 70.

of the law, but "an effulgence of human consciousness in determined transitional situations", in the words of Kafka, who would add: "It is not strictly speaking the sensible world which is appearance, it is its evil, indeed, that builds for our eyes, the sensible world".[9]

[9] F. Kafka, *Réflexions sur le péché, la souffrance, l'espérance et le vrai chemin*, traduction de B. Pautrat, Paris, Rivages poche, coll. "Petite bibliothèque", p. 63.

4

Magritte's Multiplicities and Warnier's Inspirations

Jane I Guyer
John Hopkins University, Baltimore, Maryland

Introduction

Warnier's article offers great stimulation to revisit several lines of thought about the spiritual world in everyday life. The importance of analogical thought, which he alludes to as the Magritte effect, is a very important line of enquiry into complexly turbulent day-to-day worlds. Although social life may always have had some of these dynamics, and our discipline has alluded to these, the cases Warnier presents are surprises of current daily life. I would be inspired by his paper to revisit my own lecture on "The quickening of the unknown": Epistemologies of surprise in anthropology (The Munro Lecture, 2013),[1] and my own topics on economic anthropology, to which he alludes. As he defines the Magritte effect, "all conditions are brought together to merge the discursive terms and the representations with the crisis event."

The allusion to Magritte very creatively provokes questions about how such analogical thought is done, in what terms, by whom, across times and places. The British Witchcraft Act of 1542 defined a witch as a person causing damage through

---

[1] Guyer, Jane I. 2013, "The quickening of the unknown": Epistemologies of surprise in anthropology" *HAU Journal of Ethnographic Theory* 3 (3): 283–307.

spiritual powers, for money. It was seriously condemned and punished. The Act was redefined in the eighteenth century, but only formally and completely taken off the books in the post-World War II period. So we can ask the question of how such European legal concepts operated in the colonial world.

As Warnier notes, I myself have not examined this in my own work on local economies in Nigeria and Cameroon, largely because the people themselves did not invoke what we have called "witchcraft" and "sorcery" in these contexts. Yoruba divination referred more symbolically to the place of the ancient gods of the polytheistic world, such as Eshu, the god of confusion, whose face is carved at the top of the divination tray where the cowries, beads and other items are thrown in order for the pattern to be interpreted. Certainly there are Yoruba words translated into English as "witch" (*aje*, the female version) and *oso*, the male sorcerer), but I have no field-notes on their appearance in economic life. Warnier's paper would now stimulate me to be more attentive to how such words emerge in economically related description, interpretation and discussion of causality and responsibility.

I devote my comments to a theme his paper does not yet address directly: the people's own words and their deployment. His cases raise a very provocative search into the historical nuancing of terminologies: not only in our discipline, but particularly in religious and legal texts from the past that remain relevant in situational ways in people's lives in the present, including the religious worlds to which he alludes. In the use of terms such as witchcraft, sorcery and magic, people are drawing from archives: of memory, as well as those stored in libraries and legal records. Following Warnier's mention of Pentecostalists, I searched the biblical sources and the church interpretations. What falls under the concept of sorcery has clearly shifted over thousands of years, in the translations of the texts from which the rules derive, both religious rules and the law, which in English history derived through the Anglican Church into state law and then colonial law. It would be very provocative for further thought in African Studies, to track the linguistics of this "other world": in African languages, in translations of the Bible, and in the sermonizing of the present. Allusions and quotations, as judgments, evoke and configure – like Magritte - elements from whole archives of experience and knowledge.

Words and Meanings: Sources

I: Biblical translations: It would be very interesting to trace how these key passages, used in Europe's long history of wrestling with witchcraft and sorcery, were translated into African languages. Here are two passages in the Hebrew Bible, in the books of Leviticus and Deuteronomy, that refer to occult powers and have been alluded to in the religious sources on witchcraft.

a) Leviticus 19:31

J.H. Hertz Jewish translation, from the original Hebrew. "Turn ye not unto the ghosts and the familiar spirits. Do not enquire to be defiled of them."

Hertz comments that *nefesh*, in Hebrew, is a polyvalent noun, referring to the spirit of a person, but in some contexts to a dead person or a corpse.

Robert Alter Jewish translation, from Hebrew (more recent than Hertz). "Do not turn to the ghosts, and the familiar spirits, do not enquire to be defiled of them."

Vulgate, in Latin, late 4th century

51

Uses the terms *magos* and *ariolis*.

King James Version (English, 1611)

"Regard not them that have familiar spirits, neither seek after wizards, to be defiled by them. I am the Lord your God."

b) Deuteronomy 18:10-12.

J.H. Hertz Jewish translation, from Hebrew: "There shall not be found among you anyone that maketh his son or his daughter to pass through fire, one that useth divination, a soothsayer or a diviner, or a charmer, or one that consulteth a ghost or a familiar spirit, or a necromancer For whosoever doeth these things is an abomination unto the Lord. (Hertz's commentary includes etymological reference to wizard, wise, and knowing).

Robert Alter Jewish translation, from Hebrew (more recent than Hertz), uses similar words: a speller of charms, a sorcerer, a diviner, a chanter of incantations, or an enquirer of ghosts or familiar spirits.

The King James Version of the English Bible: There shall not be found among you one that maketh his son or his daughter to pass through the fire or that useth divination or an observer of times or an enchanter or a witch. Or a charmer or consultor with familiar spirits, or a wizard or a necromancer.

Etymologically, our English words derive from a mixture of sources: witch from *wicca* (with a long history back into PIE, Proto-Indo-European); sorcerer from the French; necromancer also from old French, diviner from Latin. We see here that the words are nuanced over time. As noted, witchcraft became a legal term in England in the seventeenth century.

We can ask how these same words are now rendered in African biblical translations, prayers, proverbs, and customary-legal contexts. We can then be provoked by the concept of the Magritte Effect to explore their situational mobilization, with all the resulting dynamics of their invocation: in life and in the more public arts and performance of present day life in Africa, and elsewhere, in music, film, political speeches, sermons and other forms. The classic ethnography of African witchcraft and sorcery provides an archive of case material to explore on this crucial question of the archives for evocation and configuration on which people draw.

II. Ethnographic Sources

We have a deep archive of ethnographic sources on African terms on this domain of spiritual powers that may, or may not, be embodied in some physical form, but which can have strong material effects. Still relevant is Marwick's guidance to the study of witchcraft and sorcery as having "wide distribution among human societies... (but) in African societies (people) are more precise in their categories of the supernatural than we are." (1970:12).[2] Can we trace this "precision" as the world shifts and changes? Certainly Warnier's Magritte Effect examples will help us to reach into the disciplinary archive as a source for incidents in the ethnographic record, where different peoples, in their own languages, connect people, events and the mobilization of spiritually-based powers. In the disciplinary archive, we have specific cases from Africa, and elsewhere that witchcraft has been studied, and we might also learn from studying documented cases in European legal history. Specificity of place, time, situation and participation offers a rich source for

---

[2] Marwick, Max. 1970 Introduction. In his (ed.) *Witchcraft and Sorcery. Selected Readings*. Penguin Books, 11-18.

us for studying the archives of knowledge, experience and applicability the people are drawing on. It also encourages close attention to the local expertise designated as responsible for this work, and how are they configuring a situational Magritte Effect that infuses the current event with its own powers. We can search into the ethnographic record, as well as the philosophical and religious sources, for examples that our own discipline has been crafted to apprehend and to convey to those who were not present.

Evans-Pritchard's foundational work, *Witchcraft, Oracles and Magic among the Azande*[3], from his fieldwork in the 1920s, starts with the observation that for the Azande witchcraft is "an organic and hereditary phenomenon…. Azande believe that witchcraft is a substance in the bodies of witches". Witchcraft substance is *mangu*. It descends unilineally: "the sons of a male witch are all witches but his daughters are not, while the daughters of a female witch are all witches but her sons are not." All kinds of misfortune, and even deaths, are attributed to witches. And he gives a long list of Zande words that refer to, or invoke qualities of, *mangu* and other material-spiritual forces. Philip Mayer [4](in Marwick's edited collection, 1970) commented that such "evil powers" were seen as "embodied", generally in material forms within the human body, passed down through descent. His collection of classic sources includes twelve cases, from the Ancient World through Africanist classics, with an expanding implication that sorcery – the use of *non-human* material, rather than embodied spiritual,

[3] Evans-Pritchard, E.E. 1937. *Witchcraft, Oracles and Magic among the Azande*. Clarendon Press.

[4] Mayer, Philip. 1970 (a lecture delivered in1954). Witches. In Marwick, ed. *Witchcraft and Sorcery. Selected Readings*. Penguin Books, 45-64.

powers – is taking up greater space in the interpretation of life events.

Conclusion

Warnier's paper encourages us to re-read the classics, and to listen very closely to the people's own words, evocations, discussions in their own languages, and their, possibly differentiated and contentious, interpretations of turbulent events. Satan? Mangu? In the current world, events of the kind described by Warnier happen, by surprise, and they also, in many times and places, happen within contexts of the larger social and economic turmoil on which many of us in anthropology are now focused. This paper offers a signpost for recuperating all the sources we will need – from art such as Magritte, from translations of religious sources, from our disciplinary archive, and possibly many other sources – to engage with people's own terms for dealing with our current "ethnographic present" of the twenty-first century, with its indeterminacies in an emergent temporal register. The image of the Magritte Effect sets an example of how to do this, by opening up to the richness of analogical thinking.

5

From One Crisis to Another: Afrodystopia

Joseph Tonda
Omar Bongo University Libreville, Gabon

Jean-Pierre Warnier's text is the perfect illustration of what I call Afrodystopia, or, where shadows are reality; where anthropologists and Pentecostal pastors, fuelled with good epistemological and humanistic intentions, forge, without knowing it, Magritte's witchcraft pipe which makes of him a sorcerer. In short, reality is a diabolical machine that transforms, without your knowledge, despite your reluctance, your intentions, even negative ones, a machine that produces cognitive dissonance and madness, that is to say, a crisis of the mind or of reason without this dissonance ever ceasing to be spiritual or rational. In Afrodystopia, fathers are unknowingly husbands to their daughters, who are, at the same time, their rivals; daughters are the mothers of their mothers; children are their fathers' parents-in-law, and they are the latter's eaters[1]; wealth and success are evidence of the Devil and of God, equally; fits of madness are revealing of radical pragmatism that makes of knowledge, without ceasing to be true, or "real", not that…which produces it.

My Congolese childhood was profoundly marked by this Afrodystopian machine. This took place during a long and collective witchcraft crisis that occurred in the 1950s and which unfurled beyond the states of Congo and Gabon, by way of the

---

[1] I refer to the phenomenon of "child sorcerers".

anti-witchcraft cult of Mademoiselle. In 1957 the prophets of Mademoiselle, who exercised incredible physical violence against family heads and even against children in the name of the fight against witchcraft – *izanga* and *ngoye* (the panther) –, wanted, in front of a crowd gathered in the village where we lived, to make me eat cassava. Monsignor Pascal Zoaka Zoaka, one of the great prophets of this cult, and his lieutenants failed miserably, faced with my refusal to eat that thing which I loathed, despite their incantations, their demonstrations of physical force. Which provoked screams of fear of the peasantry gathered around: *"Otè mwana a n'izanga!"* (This child has witchcraft in him). *Izanga* is witchcraft, and mine manifested in the disappointment that I had inflicted upon the anti-sorcerer prophets. I was 5 years old. To this day I do not eat cassava, even though they had prophesied otherwise. It is both as a researcher and a member of hundreds of African families that go through this experience that my revolt against this whole social phenomenon unfolds in my research today. What I hold of this double experience that imposed itself onto me is that the witchcraft "crisis" must be apprehended through the sociological lens, with, as prospect, the questioning of the status of reality in African societies. What is reality? What is the reality of the "witchcraft crisis?"

One example will suffice: as I finish writing the first version of this article, that Sunday of the 29th of October 2017, I am informed of a family reunion at my nephew's (who is only 2 years older than me) home in the Nzeng-Ayong quarter of Libreville. The reunion focuses on his wife's "fits of madness" (that is what I am told, in French, over the phone). A former senator, now retired, my nephew, the son of my sister who passed away 4 years ago, graduated from IEP Grenoble, where he studied "Eco-Fi". It is after having worked for a while as

58

procurator in a bank, then as executive director and financial assistant at Gabon's Water and Energy Company (the *Société d'eau et d'énergie du Gabon* – *SEEG*) that he entered politics and was elected as senator in 2007. He is father to 30 children (this is not counting those who are not known of) and is legally married to M.M., who is plagued by "fits of madness." M.M. is the mother of four of the children in my nephew's huge phratry. The eldest of M.M's children passed away 9 months prior, at the age of 24. He suffered from sickle cell anaemia (SCA). His mother, brothers and sisters, and his mother's side of the family knew that he was afflicted with this disease. M.M. is from the matrilinear Punu ethnic group. My nephew and I are from the Mahongwé ethnic group, part of what is called in Gabon, Kota, and we are patrilineal. A dispute over the rituals that had been performed to separate us from the deceased child kept apart our family and that of S.Y.'s (my nephew's) wife. M.M.'s (S.Y.'s wife's) maternal side of the family imposed their Punu rituals with an irrefutable argument: when my nephew went on to marry M.M., he submitted to the Punu marital codes. These are the same codes that apply in the event of death. These are the codes of the real father of the child, who is M.M.'s brother. It is to be noted here that this real father considers his sister's children as his "things", his "goats", which he can dispose of at will. In witchcraft, he can "eat" them. My nephew is, according to the codes of matrilinear lineage, the "guardian" of the children of his cannibalistic slave master (symbolic) of a brother-in-law, who is, from this point of view, his "rival", but also his "wife" because the wife's brother is his brother-in-law's man-wife. I refer, for a detailed presentation of the codes of matrilinear lineage, Patrice Yengo's excellent book.[2]

It is during my sojourn in France, from the 16th to the 18th of October 2017, that M.M.'s "fits of madness" occurred. These comprised, for example, of attempts to strangle my nephew in his sleep. The couple's children, with L.Y., M.M.'s first bon daughter, at their head, took the side of "their" family, i.e. their mother's side, whose leaders are their maternal uncles. Children, maternal uncles and the mother's sisters then publicly accused my nephew of being responsible for his wife's "fits of madness". According to them, S.Y. is a Rosicrucian sorcerer doubling as practitioner of "pygmy medicine" and of the potent *teke-obamba* "drug" called *Ndjobi*. The "drugs" are what are also called "fetishes". Along with this, M.M.'s family blames S.Y. for being stingy: "You are rich, you do not give us money, you even let your wife's first child die, because you did not love him", say his in-laws, in whose midst are his children. His eldest daughter, then taking on the role of anti-witchcraft prophet who wanted me to eat cassava and failed at it, is at the forefront of this anti-witchcraft crusade against her father! In the diabolically pragmatic logic of his accusers, there is obviously only one with the evil heart, that is to say, who is a sorcerer, behaving as does my nephew. As so, my nephew's wealth, his Rosicrucian witchcraft, which is practised in lodges, his African drugs, which, according to representations, bear all the characteristics that require human sacrifice, are the cause of the death of the son that he raised with M.M. and the latter's "fits of madness". Sacrifice consists of the exploitation of intelligence, spirits, chance, the stars, the energies of those family members initiated into this. On this subject, initiation is,

---

[2] P. Yengo, *Les mutations sorcières dans le bassin du Congo. Du ventre et de sa politique*, Paris, Karthala, 2016.

in Gabon, key word, fetish word, which takes over the minds of peoples, regardless of their social class. This takeover is consubstantial with the violence of the imaginary on ritual crimes in the country. But the key word that is initiation forms part of a whole society of key words that possesses peoples and is composed around Rosicrucianism, Freemasonry, the devil, energies, the stars, spirits, the spiritual realm, chance, ritual crimes, etc.... In Gabon, this society informed by words works in the minds of people as money does.[3] Let us remember that S.Y.'s family-in-law blames him for not sharing his wealth, which materialises in the form of money. In short, my nephew is accused by a coalition of his children and parents-in-law, possessed by a society of fetish words fashionable at the time, having sacrificed his wife so as to "work" with her "mind", since her troubles are "spiritual". My nephew is thus socially shaped by the despotism of a society of spirit words, fetish words, as a mind "eater", that is to say, a sorcerer, and that is why his daughter, who has a law degree and is currently training at a solicitors' firm, and to whom I have unwisely dedicated my most recent novel as a manner of encouraging her toward success (I will come back to this in a moment), requires that her father take his wife to the church where pray both women: mother and daughter. My nephew refuses, resists, and wants to take his wife to the hospital. His daughter and her real family make the final decision and M.M. is taken to the Pentecostal church. The pastor has revelations to make: my nephew carries evil spirits with him; the devil came into his life when he was just a child because he was raised by an aunt. S.Y. disputes this: he was never raised by an aunt. Even then, he is held responsible for his wife's illness, and must confess his sins. The

---

[3] J. Tonda, *L'impérialisme postcolonial. Critique de la société des éblouissements*, Paris, Karthala, 2015.

pressure is so strong that he must confess, but what? His adulteries, yes, there are "many women". The pastor places his hands onto him, asks him to convert so as to free his wife from the clutches of his evil spirits, which his body is home to. Four days after "deliverance" sessions, to which S.Y. participates, M.M. is still not calm. She is even more agitated, more aggressive, more violent. Her daughter then demands that her father takes her mother to the hospital. My nephew, who could not have asked for better, complies. The anamnesis leads to the conclusion of a "deep depression". Treatment is given; M.M. calms down after one day of treatment. I see her at the reunion on that Sunday, 29th of October. She has lost a lot of weight, but still sits in the living room of their home. She kisses me as I arrive and asks about my "home" (my family). She will take part in the meeting at which everything that I have just described was said.

The most interesting thing about this Afrodystopian machine is this: in the real family of my nephew's daughter, L.Y, who is leading this anti-witchcraft crusade against her father, as well as in his family, everyone knows that the deceased not only suffered from sickle cell anaemia, but that he was also the biological son of another man; that M.M.'s mother, who passed away 10 years earlier, was mad and that she had been abandoned by her family, at my nephew's, S.Y.'s, home. Everyone knew that, but this knowledge is turned by the power of the *id* ("the social unconscious") of the social realm into accessory. Real knowledge, knowledge of the real, which is knowledge of the principle of synthesis, then shows reality differently from what it is. That is why the dedication that I make in my novel to M.M. and S.Y.'s daughter may bring upon me accusation of witchcraft. I publicly asked, at the last reunion on the 29th of October, that I be allowed to have a discussion with my niece, for failing to destroy all copies of my novel. I was dissuaded from doing so: despite my good intentions, such a move would have been interpreted as a way of exonerating myself from an evil act. Another detail, which is important about these "fits of madness", is as follows: my nephew's strong protest against him being accused of witchcraft received, amongst others, this response from one of his sisters-in-law: "Who do you want me to accuse for my sister's illness?" We can only condemn you, you are her husband; and the death or illness of a wife are always attributed to the action of her husband, and vice versa." A couple, a husband and his wife, thus find themselves within a configuration of "structural accusation." The question, epistemological, which poses itself, is this: in which genus should we put this "structural accusation"? In the genus of "representations", "the imaginary", "rumour", "gossip" or in that of pragmatism? Can we think of the pragmatic beyond the current Afrodystopian episteme?

Jean-Pierre Warnier says in his article that the economic surveys do not indicate the presence of witchcraft in the economic activity of Africans. He tells us that all is not witchcraft in Africa and that people act in a pragmatic manner. Is this a way of saying that in terms of accusation of witchcraft, pragmatism is absent? It seems to me that the "M.M. case" that I have just described, and which is still developing as I write this, makes difficult, if not impossible, the separation between the "representations", the "imaginary" on the one hand, and "crises" on the other. For, representations and crises are inseparable from interpretations and the questions that form part of the reality that produce the Afrodystopian machine symbolised by the *id*, the social unconscious. Furthermore, what inspires us not only in the "M.M. case" but also in my own empirical experience of "witchcraft crises" is the fact that these are absolutely not rare. It would suffice, from a methodological point of view, to ask each colleague from a Central African university, or each student, if they have an experience of these "crises", to understand that they are part of the more or less traumatic experiences in their lives. In writing this text, I am aware of being trapped into the Afrosystopian machine that is expressed by way of this Nzebi proverb from Gabon: each death has an owner.

6

The Incompleteness of the African Subject

Francis B. Nyamnjoh
University of Cape Town, South Africa

William Arens published in 1979 *The Man-eating Myth*.[1] In this book he took to task the provability, prevalent in anthropological circles, of anthropophagy or what is popularly known as cannibalism since Christopher Columbus' 15th century voyage of "discovery" of the Caribbean and related geographies. Arens argued that cannibalism, as extravagantly represented in creative and scholarly accounts of European encounters with the rest of the world, was pure fabrication, a figment of European imagination, and a projection of Europe's civilizational claims and its ambitions of conquest and dominance over nature and other cultures. Arens's book generated and continues to generate heated controversy. While many scholars have taken issue with his sweeping and categorically dismissal of cannibalism, few would question Arens's challenge to scholars to authenticate and substantiate more and with actual empirical evidence than merely to claim, evoke or insinuate the existence of cannibalism and its normalcy in many a so-called primitive society prior to contact with the prescriptive evangelical enlightenment gaze of Europe.

---

[1] Arens, W. (1979) *The Man-eating Myth*, New York: Oxford University Press.

Jean-Pierre Warnier's 2017 paper *"Ceci n'est pas un sorcier: l'effet Ma*gritte en sorcellerie*"* ("This is not a witch. About the Magritte effect in matters of witchcraft")[2] raises similar objections to the proliferation, with evangelical zeal, of scholarly representations of witchcraft in Africa, taking especial exception to some of the scholarship that would like to pass for evidence of the assumed normalcy of witchcraft on the continent. Warnier is however not as categorical in his dismissal of claims of witchcraft as Arens was of cannibalism. He believes there may well be a baby in the bathwater of witchcraft studies worth saving, but to save that baby requires effort and investment in conceptual and methodological rigour of the best traditions of the observational field sciences.

Warnier uses to good effect the analogy of the reality of traffic accidents in France, which results in 3500 deaths annually. Also effective is his discussion of the popular imagination and representations that accompany the phenomenon, and the daily efforts by 66 million Frenchmen and women to take precautions to minimise such traffic accidents and their effects. He argues that the reality of witchcraft in Africa is no different, despite its purported ubiquity as an overarching belief system and an organising logic of social interactions.

Warnier challenges scholars of witchcraft to – in the manner of a sociologist of traffic accidents in France – demonstrate a more rigorous sense of evidence through meticulous, methodical, systematic empirical substantiation of what he terms actual cases of *"la crise sorcellaire paroxystique"* ("the paroxystic crises of witchcraft"). Such evidence should, in the manner of good ethnography, be characterised by "thick

---

[2] Warnier, J.-P. (2017) "Ceci n'est pas un sorcier: l'effet Magritte en sorcellerie," *Politique Africaine*, No. 146. Pp. 125-141.

description" as opposed to "thin" or "no" description. If the baby of witchcraft studies must survive, scholars in the field can ill afford to simply fall back on prevalent popular witchcraft discourses and representations, with the flimsy excuse that witchcraft is rather difficult to prove empirically. The test of any theoretical pudding is in the practical eating, he insists. This should be no different in witchcraft studies.

Empirical provability of witchcraft is doable, even if it is a tall order. Warnier illustrates how, with three cases – the only such cases he witnessed in his over 45 years of active participation as an anthropologist and ethnographer in Cameroon – of "witchcraft crisis". Some might argue that his personal experience of only three cases of witchcraft in action by no means implies the paucity of the phenomenon, especially given that his main research focus was not pointedly on and around issues of witchcraft. If the statement *"Toi, tu es un blanc. Tu es en dehors de ça"* ("You, you are white. You are outside of it") (p. 131), by Jean, his witchcraft afflicted colleague at the University of Yaounde, is anything to go by, then perhaps Warnier's Cameroonian associates tended to insulate him from their witchcraft headaches, because he was white. That said, in view of the noted tendency for witchcraft accusations to take place within the intimate circles of kin[3], it could be argued that Jean took Warnier into confidence precisely because the latter was a white man, and not in spite of that. As such, he saw Warnier as a harmless outsider who could be a therapeutic confidante, and not a danger or a risk. One could assume that this was the case in other instances like that of the mechanic, Oyono, who found it easier to share their predicaments with him than with other Cameroonians.

---

[3] Geschiere, P. (2013) *Witchcraft, Intimacy, and Trust: Africa in Comparison*, Chicago: University of Chicago Press.

Even if the cases of witchcraft Warnier encountered during his 45 years in Cameroon were, like the analogy of 3500 deaths a year from traffic accidents in France that he provides, his argument would still be valid: that it is necessary to avoid sweeping and simplistic generalisations from limited observations and that it is always better to describe than to represent in the abstract. Perhaps, in recognition of the fact of his rather limited experience with describable cases of "*la crise sorcellaire*", Warnier summons as evidence the added example of 11 out of 1000 cases of autopsies associated with witchcraft in a western Cameroon anthropology doctoral study of 2009 by M. Salpeteur. The systematic documentation of court cases pertaining to witchcraft by Cyprian Fisiy is also used as added evidence that it is possible to measure, scientifically and quantitatively, actual cases of witchcraft rather than simply contenting oneself with a generalised qualitative discourse analysis to the effect that Africa is one vast dark forest of witchcraft afflictions. Warnier seems to suggest, and rightly so, that we do neither science nor Africa any good with extravagant and thinly substantiated claims about witchcraft among Africans, regardless of social status or background. If reaching for the skies is the goal of witchcraft studies, those involved in such ambitions must do so with their feet firmly grounded in and on the observable empirical dimensions of their claims.

I am mostly in agreement with Warnier's call for scientific rigour and empirical evidence, a point I made in a recent discussion of public anthropology.[4] To add to his analogy of traffic deaths in France, I would say that in studying witchcraft

---

[4] Nyamnjoh, F. B. (2015) "Beyond an evangelising public anthropology: Science, theory and commitment," *Journal of Contemporary African Studies*, 33(1): 48-63.

as a technology of self-extension in Africa, researchers must desist from the syndrome of a worker whose only tool is a hammer and to whom every problem is a nail. A science or scholarship that dramatizes the hammer when many other technologies/tools are begging for attention, recognition and relevance does no justice to the multifaceted and nuanced complexities of social reality. Just as those who resort to witchcraft discourses in their daily existence (or talk about traffic accidents) are not in a permanent state of enchantment by its magic (and reality), scholars/students of society should desist from the one-dimensionalism that would seem to suggest that witchcraft is or could be a one-stop shop in a zero sum game of winner takes all in being African and in knowing Africa. Such an approach to science and knowledge is bounded, totalising, totalitarian and at the mercy and service of ideology.

I would like to conclude with an epistemological relevance of popular beliefs in of witchcraft and sorcery[5] which Warnier does not delve into in the current paper, an idea I develop in greater detail in a book on what Amos Tutuola teaches us about the fluidity and flexibility of reality and personhood in Africa.[6] If one does not simply dismiss or explain such phenomena and occurrences under the label of witchcraft, magic, occult or superstition, the proliferation of unusual or unnatural happenings in Tutuola's novels suddenly takes on a whole new meaning epistemologically. In his novels, Tutuola seeks to reassure his readers that it is possible to be what

---

[5] Nyamnjoh, F. B. (2001) "Delusions of development and the enrichment of witchcraft discourses in Cameroon," In: Moore H, Sanders T (eds) *Magical Interpretations, Material Realities: Modernity, Witchcraft and the Occult in Postcolonial Africa*, London: Routledge, 28-49.

[6] Nyamnjoh, F. B. (2017) *Drinking from the Cosmic Gourd: How Amos Tutuola Can Change Our Minds*, Bamenda: Langaa.

Charles Taylor terms "open and porous and vulnerable" to a world of spirits, powers and cosmic forces, and still be "disenchanted" enough to have the confidence of Taylor's "buffered self," exploring one's own "powers of moral ordering".[7] The emphasis on the negativity of so-called witchcraft and sorcery in Africa has tended to de-emphasise the epistemological potential of belief systems and practices that refuse to caricature reality through resorting to easy dichotomies between ways of being and knowing by means of sensory perception and other forms of being and knowing that are not easily reducible to the senses and linear conceptions of time and space.

To achieve a much more fruitful epistemological turn, African social scientists (practicing and aspirant) and practitioners of the humanities would have to turn to and seek to be cultivated afresh by ordinary Africans immersed in popular traditions of meaning making steeped in popular epistemologies of inclusivity, interconnection, and interdependence.

---

[7] Taylor, C. (2007) *A Secular Age*, Cambridge Massachusetts: Belknap of Harvard University Press.

Witchcraft: A Knowledge that Defies Knowing?

Peter Geschiere
University of Amsterdam, The Netherlands

Over the last years Jean-Pierre Warnier seems to like reversals. He is the author of most evocative pages on the plight of young men in the Grassfields societies, many of them excluded from marriage and even sex, destined to remain juniors for all their life, and therefore forming a rebellious but more or less hidden counterpoint in these tightly organised societies. But a few years ago, shifting from Marx to Foucault, he rather emphasised the deep commitment of the same youngsters to their chiefs, accepting the blessing with his saliva as a proper reward for their collaboration. In his present text there is a similar volte-face.[1] With his 1988 article, together with Michael Rowlands,[2] he has been one of the forerunners of the comeback of "witchcraft" as a central topic in anthropology and African studies, after a relative neglect during the first post-Independence decades. But in the present text he warns that there is a growing and worrying discrepancy between the omnipresence of this topic in recent academic literature and everyday life where, at least in his experience, real witchcraft crises are relatively rare.

His rich ethnography in *Régner au Cameroun* shows that there is good reason for the first reversal mentioned. His last

---

[1] J.-P. Warnier, *Régner au Cameroun. Le Roi-Pot*, Paris: Karthala, 2009.

[2] M. Rowlands and J.-P. Warnier, "Sorcery, Power and the Modern State in Cameroun," *Man* 1988, vol. 23, 3: 118-132.

text on witchcraft is much shorter, but there also I see good reason for some more reflection on what the return of witchcraft in anthropological studies does. The tortuous trajectory of the topic over the last decades in this discipline is indeed somewhat worrying.[3] While it used to be a fixed beacon in classical anthropological studies, it quite suddenly disappeared after 1960 from the discipline's agenda (more completely in the Anglophone literature than in the Francophone). An obvious reason was that it became politically incorrect at the time when people celebrated the "the young states of Africa" and anthropology had to defend itself against the criticism of having been "colonialism's handmaiden," always intent on "primitivising Africa." However, the 1990's brought the spectacular return of the topic in a context of general disappointment about modernisation and development. Since then the topic is again omnipresent in anthropological studies. And it is, indeed, the renewed popularity of the topic that justifies some worries about the effects of our use of the term: to what extent do academic studies thus contribute to make popular worries about a supposed proliferation of witchcraft a self-fulfilling prophecy?[4]

Moreover, I certainly share Warnier's warnings against a tendency in at least some studies to rely on interviews and discourse. I agree that it is vital to follow how ideas about witchcraft are acted out in practice. Only when the research is based on a solid analysis of everyday events and their sometimes highly complicated ramifications in space and in

---

[3] See P. Geschiere, *The Modernity of Witchcraft, Power and the Occult in Postcolonial Africa*, University of Virginia Press, 1997.

[4] See P. Geschiere, *Witchcraft, Intimacy and Trust, Africa in Comparison*, University of Chicago Press, 2013.

time, can we gain insight in the way people "work" with these general notions, their inconsistencies and ambivalent meanings. It is only in such concrete settings that omnipresent scepticism – people's determined efforts to unmask charlatans – can come into the picture. Following rumours and stories can easily create the impression of a general credulity for which anything goes; only by following how such ideas are acted out can people's often sophisticated ways of testing certain claims be brought out.

But there are also points where I would be less inclined to follow Warnier. First of all, I think it is important to emphasise that Africa is not so exceptional in this respect. As I tried to show in the comparative chapters of my 2013 book, terms like "witchcraft" are omnipresent in everyday life in many parts of the globe. Of course in Melanesia – in anthropological literature often mentioned as some sort of complement to Africa in its preoccupation with witchcraft.[5] But also in many parts of Asia, Latin America, and even Europe. The relevance of Jean and John Comaroff's notion of "occult economies" is precisely that these magical aspects emerge all over the globe as a fixed by-product of "millennial capitalism," not only in Africa.[6]

I must confess also some surprise that Warnier, during his long and intensive years in Cameroon, only stumbled upon three witchcraft crises. The problem here might be also the term witchcraft, which keeps haunting our studies of this aspect of life. Most colleagues will agree that it is a very bad translation of local notions. However, it has been so generally

---

[5] Cf. K. Rio, M. MacCarthy and R. Blanes, eds, *Pentecostalism and Witchcraft, Spiritual Warfare in Africa and Melanesia*, Palgrave-Macmillan, 2017.

[6] J. and J. Comaroff, "Millennial Capitalism: First Thoughts on a Second Coming," *Public Culture* 12:291-344 (2000).

appropriated throughout the African continent (as elsewhere) that it is difficult to avoid. The issue might be less that it is a bad translation – after all, translations are productive, as Birgit Meyer has reminded us – but rather the extreme openness of the term. It is becoming ever more a panacea that easily acquires the qualities of a self-fulfilling prophecy: if everything is witchcraft, then indeed witchcraft is everywhere. However, I wonder whether the solution is then to try and limit the term, as Warnier seems to do by recognising only three witchcraft crises. The danger is then to overlook the pervasiveness of the notion – its capacity to turn up in any context –, and it is precisely this fluidity that seems to be the secret of the resilience of these notions, despite deep changes. The limitations of the witchcraft studies of the Manchester school of the 1950s and 1960s with their focus on accusations, inspiring a vision of witchcraft as "domesticated" and reinforcing the social order, might be a warning in this respect.[7]

Neither do I think, it is very meaningful that witchcraft does not figure in studies like Janet McGaffey's on Congolese transcontinental entrepreneurship or in Jane Guyer's analysis of "marginal gains" as special to African economies. At least for the *sapeurs* we know that *le mystique* is everywhere. And Guyer's notions – like "multiple self-realisation" as typical for Equatorial African political economies or the very notion of "marginal gains" – are wide open to occult implications. I certainly agree that witchcraft logics are not the only logics to which people in Africa refer in order to deal with the rapidly changing present-day realities. But I do not think that accepting the omnipresence of witchcraft notions as one way – and apparently a quite seductive way – to interpret these

---

[7] M. Douglas, "Introduction" in *Witchcraft Confessions and Accusations*, London: Tavistock, 1970. p. xiii - xxxviii

74

changes, excludes the possibility of producing very insightful analysis of what is going on in Africa that follow other logics and ways of knowing. Most people will agree now that Freemasons and their more or less hidden networks were very important to the functioning of the Third Republic in France. But this certainly does not exclude that historical studies analysing its functioning along different logics miss the boat.

However, my main doubts concern Warnier's introducing quantification as the solution. Of course, whenever it is possible, it is good to quantify. But the problem will be time and again that this will demand fixing the fluid presence of "witchcraft" by identifying concrete pegs – such as public accusations – in order to have something to count. The quantitative turn in some of the work by historians on early modern Europe resulted in such a fixation: focus on accusations (also because juridical archives are the main source) and less interest in the fluidity of the beliefs, their ambiguous implications and their omnipresence in these historical settings as well. It is striking that the best work – at least the work that might be especially inspiring for anthropologists, like Robisheaux's magnificent analysis of one case study[8] – was not part of this quantifying turn. Rather this book explores step-by-step when the term witchcraft is emerging from the stream of rumours and gossip – contested and differently interpreted – and then how it is picked up by the lawyers and priests, and how it finally, after much struggle, comes to serve as the overall explication of the events.

For me this is also an example how to find a way-out of the present-day dilemma of witchcraft studies in Africa – that is, "witchcraft" is an unavoidable presence nowadays, yet using

---

[8] T. Robisheaux, *The Last Witch of Langenberg: Murder in a German Village*, New York: Norton, 2009.

the very term helps to turn it into a self-fulfilling prophecy. My solution would rather be combining a focus on the kaleidoscopic history of the term with detailed studies of present-day cases. One way to relativise the apparent self-evidence of the term in many settings is to study in detail how the term was introduced in a particular region and how it took root. Work by Florence Bernault and Andrea Ceriana on how the term was imported during colonial times in Gabon and the Central African Republic as some sort of working misunderstanding has pioneering qualities in this respect.[9] Incidentally both authors show also that there is good reason to be sceptical about the tendency of anthropologists to exaggerate their role in such misunderstandings – a common trend when anthropologists give in to self-reflexivity. In these colonial debates anthropologists and their choice of terms only played a minor role next to the much more powerful presence of missionaries, civil servants and doctors.

On a more micro-level similar questions could be raised in the context of grounded case studies starting from events in everyday life: when did the term witchcraft emerge in a conflict, who launched it and who contested it? Which different interpretations proved to be possible and what kind of solutions were proposed? Of course, cases where the tortuous trajectories of the word could have emerged but then were discarded again, or cases where the coming up and evaporating of the word could be followed over a longer sequence of time will be especially valuable.

---

[9] F. Bernault, "De la modernité comme impuissance: Fétichisme et crise du politique en Afrique équatoriale et ailleurs, *Cahiers d'Études africaines* 49, 3: 747-74 (2009). A. Creriane Manéri, *Sorcellerie et prophétisme en Centraafrique: L'imaginaire de la dépossesion en pays banda,* Paris: Karthala.See also H.Behrend, 2011, *Resurrecting Cannibals: The Catholic Church, Witch-Hunts & the Production of Pagans in Western Uganda.* Woodbridge: Currey, 2011.

However, this will certainly not be a final solution. The basic challenge of a notion like witchcraft – and probably the reason of people's fascination with it, also in the West – is that it promises knowledge about something that does not want to be known. Academics are supposed to make things accessible by ordering them. But, "witchcraft" derives its special power precisely from its disorder. Michael Taussig summarised this dilemma most cogently by his insistence on the power of "the murky."[10] Jim Siegel analyses the notion of the witch as a term that makes closure impossible; evoking the notion is therefore a futile attempt to come to terms with the uncanny.[11] Both approaches have the merit to help to "désenclaver l'Afrique," as Mbembe keeps admonishing us to do: witchcraft not as an African particularity but as a struggle with basic human problems. Jean-Pierre Warnier is certainly right that academics must be careful when using terms like witchcraft. We may have to do it, but reflection on the implications are most urgent.

---

[10] M. Taussig, *Shamanism, Colonialism and the Wild Man: A Study of Terror and Healing,* University of Chicago Press, 1987.

[11] J. Siegel, *Naming the Witch.* Stanford: Stanford U.P., 2006.

PART III

8

The Unfathomable Lightness of the Witch

Jean-Pierre Warnier
Imaf (Institut des mondes africains), Paris

In the last twenty years, a consensus emerged around the following points: witchcraft is plural and multifaceted; accordingly any attempt at defining it is bound to fail; one has to address it from different angles; under various guises, it is to be found all over the world (that is, it is by no means the preserve of Africa); lastly, just like kinship, religion and other kinds of social facts, it is a historical phenomenon. We have gone far past those debates. My article[1] did not address them. Pass your way; in that respect there is (almost) nothing to be seen.

All the rest is an object for debates. We shall not conclude them now and here. But it may be possible at least to peg the field thanks to the six remarkable critical comments on my article, for which I wholeheartedly thank their authors. On one point only do we seem to reach an agreement: all of us are somewhat ill at ease with the proliferation of statements and publications on that topic from quite different quarters – media, evangelical or academic. Yet one more film, recently produced (*I am not a witch*)[2], provides such an image of Africa to the voyeurism of the Western gaze.

---

[1] "Ceci n'est pas un sorcier. De l'effet Magritte en sorcellerie", *Politique africaine*, n° 146, 2017, p. 125-141.

[2] *I am not a Witch*, film by Rungano Nyomi, May 2017.

But we still have a number of points open to debate: first the frequency, prevalence and count of witchcraft occurrences. In this respect, Julien Bonhomme, Joseph Tonda and Peter Geschiere voice an informed scepticism. Nevertheless, if the seven of us were to sit together around a table, it would probably be possible for us to reach an agreement on the following: the difficulty to grasp the phenomenon, the unreliability of patchy sources, the need for a hermeneutic approach (Patrice Yengo) that resists any kind of quantitative assessment, the distinction to be made between two statements: "I have not seen anything", and "there is nothing to be seen" that do not carry the same meaning and implications. Insofar as the seven of us agree on the historical dimension of the phenomenon, we reckon that witchcraft is not an essence but an event. Its prevalence varies to a great extent depending on location, time and historical setting. We could perhaps agree on significant differences, even in the middle term, let us say between different regions of Cameroon in the 1970s and 80s, the Congo basin between 1950 and 2000 (Joseph Tonda), Central Africa and Senegal. It would allow us to avoid any misconstrued generalization from one dated local experience to the next. Enough of that!

In my article, I have wished to raise another debate – a most important one in my view -, that of the empirical basis one has to obtain in any attempt at a historical and anthropological analysis; in other words, that of the ethnographic object. Collecting a genealogy, a technical process, a market transaction, an initiation ritual rests on a number of relatively tangible and objectifiable elements concerning names, kinship relationships, material devices, currency, gestures and words.

This is not the case in matters of witchcraft. It is polymorphous, difficult to grasp, inscribed in discursive practices that are to a large extent performative and circular. Is it possible to secure any tangible element on which the ethnographer can lean and avoid losing its balance in such quicksand? I have organized my discussion around the Magritte effect in order to expose and criticize the easiest ethnographic option, and in my view the least relevant one, that consists in collapsing together the thing (the presumed action of the witch) and its representation – especially discursive – and to take at face value only the verbal statements, without further discriminating between different kinds of speech acts and contexts.

And God knows that the discourse of and about witchcraft may be as delirious as it is garrulous. My argument elicits a certain amount of scepticism with several colleagues. Peter Geschiere underscores the main reason for this: what is characteristic of all forms of witchcraft is the fact that they belong with the occult and are difficult to grasp and objectify. This is precisely the drive behind their efficacy and power in social life. It is the "id" of Joseph Tonda. By its very nature, any conspiracy theory is impossible to verify or to falsify. It does not lend itself to any ethnographic enquiry in the usual sense of the term. Witchcraft stands at the border of the real and can easily push us beyond the limit, and out of the domain defined by the ambition of the social sciences. It invites one to learn something that repels knowledge. It is a unique ethnographic object that should be approached by the researcher only at the cost of the most exacting methodological sophistication. If we agree on such an observation, we do not necessarily reach the same conclusions as regards the kind of ethnography that it recommends. Joseph Tonda rejects my suggestions as so many illustrations of an Afrodystopia.

Given the prolixity and performative potential of the witchcraft discourse, the option that recommends itself to the researcher is to conduct an ethnography of discursive practice. Julien Bonhomme explores that option by identifying three types of discourse: common representations, public narratives conveyed by the media or by hearsay, and intimate stories in which the ethnographer is involved as a first-hand witness and even as an agent. Given the fact that these three types of discourse feed into one another, Julien Bonhomme recommends studying the dynamics of circulation, the speech conditions and the forms of the ethnographer's implication. He has brilliantly illustrated this program in his last books. Researchers would be well advised to follow his lead.

Within the perimeter delimited by such an option, Jane Guyer suggests analysing the lexemes in use, their historical origins, their translation from one language to another, and to assess the performative impact of such transpositions. On his side, Patrice Yengo proposes a hermeneutic approach to enunciation that seems to be required in such matters, with the striking example of the nun hit by a *fulla-fulla* at Pointe Noire. It illustrates the sudden capsizing of the meaning of given statements depending on the different modes and contexts of knowledge, especially thanks to analogical thought, as Jane Guyer says. Joseph Tonda's narrative also takes place in the category of Julien Bonhomme's intimate stories. I personally am in agreement with Patrick Yengo's proposal and the third option of Julien Bonhomme as validated by Peter Geschiere when he recommends to pay special attention to daily life: namely an ethnography of the embedded discourse, to which I would add up (on top of it and not instead of) that of the bodily conducts and the materialities - essential to the witchcraft crisis -, not for their sign value in a system of connotation and communication, but for their praxic value in a system of agency, that is, for what they do to the subject, to his body, his psyche, his belongings, his relationships to others. This proposal necessitates making use of a praxeological grid of analysis in addition to the structuralist, semiotic or discourse analysis ones. In that domain, there exists a factor of tangible efficacy. Moreover, most of the time, there exists a cognitive gap between the discourse and the embodied experience that constitutes, in my view, an essential factor of compliance to the universe of witchcraft[3]. On this topic, there is food for more debate, presumably for a long time.

Francis Nyamnjoh considers witchcraft as one more particular case of the incompleteness of the African as narrated by the Nigerian writer Amos Tutuola. He underscores the fluidity and flexibility of the real and of the person in Africa that validates the epistemological relevance of popular beliefs concerning human beings – open, porous, vulnerable to anything that is other and different from self. The subject finds an extension in the living and the dead, the parents, the dead elders, diverse beings such as animals and spirits. One would yield once more to the Magritte effect if one were to limit oneself to verbal statements in such matters. This is not the case with Tutuola and Francis Nyamnjoh since they bring into the picture many bodily practices that testify of the imprint of lived incompleteness, such as those concerning the relationship to elders, ancestors, divination, and everything that belongs with witchcraft in the broad sense of the term. In

---

[3] See U. Mohan and J.-P Warnier, "Marching the devotional subject: The bodily-and-material cultures of religion", *Journal of Material Culture*, 2017, Vol. 22(4) 369–384.

my opinion, this worldview has the enormous advantage of being Lacan and Foucault-compatible insofar as it reveals that, in social practice, the subject is never where s/he thinks s/he is, that it is multiple, that it governs itself but is equally the object of the other's actions on its own conducts, even without his knowledge; that it is incomplete, at the same time autonomous and heteronomous, unstable, shaped by others than self, vulnerable, contingent; This very notion of a porous subject contrasts sharply with that – so misleading – of the individual, sole manager of him/herself, as put forward by economic science and mainstream social sciences in the Western world. This theme merges with that of witchcraft as a murky thing mentioned by Peter Geschiere.

This approach to the incompleteness and its witchcraft corollary also has the great advantage of putting on an equal footing African popular epistemologies (mentioned by Francis Nyamnjoh and Joseph Tonda) and the scholarly discourse concerning the unstable and porous subject, and to build up bridges between them, failing what the narrative on witchcraft could be brought down to the level of a delirium that the sceptical scholar could dismiss without complying or feeling implicated at all, thus yielding to his/her Afrodystopic leanings. Accordingly, I would dare to say that, from within the implicated enunciation (as analysed by Julien Bonhomme), I do subscribe to the witchcraft narrative (as does Jeanne Favret-Saada). It means that, as a Foucauldian anthropologist, I can consent to what my colleague John tells me of his being bewitched, at the cost of the hermeneutic exercise put forward by Patrice Yengo. I express in terms of an anthropology of the subject what he says in terms of popular epistemology, with an equivalent compliance on both sides. I am aware of the tangible efficacy this episode has on him (and on myself who has been caught willy-nilly in the action and efficiently cooperates with him, his wife and his traditional practitioner). Of course, this is a matter for debate. There is no consensus on that point.

In my article on the Magritte effect, my intention has been to launch two other debates, one on research ethics in the social sciences, because the proliferation of publications on witchcraft seems to draw the social scientist on the side of the media and the evangelical preachers. This situation raises an ethical problem, pinpointed by Alban Bensa and recognized by Peter Geschiere, Julien Bonhomme and Francis Nyamnjoh. Geschiere reckons that the very small public surface occupied by the social sciences shields them from such an impact. This is probably the case and, although we have reasons to regret it, it is fortunate enough. But the question raised by Alban Bensa is grounded in the qualitative authority of the scholarly security willy-nilly granted to the common representations and to public narratives conveyed by the media and the preachers, independently from the amount of space they occupy in the public debate. It seems to me that this discussion remains more or less untouched and open. The other debate concerns the articulation between a historical sociology of politics and the researches in economy grounded in empirical enquiries from which witchcraft seems to be conspicuously absent on the one hand, and an analysis of the forms of enunciation on the other hand. It is the problem raised by the statement of Emmanuel Kamden: success in business is due to hard work and not to occult practice. Is it possible to bridge the gap between Jane Guyer ("I have not seen anything (…) largely because people themselves did not invoke what we have called "witchcraft" and "sorcery" in that context") and Emmanuel Kamden ("there is nothing to be seen")? Joseph Tonda rejects this

87

debate: "is it possible to think about pragmatics independently from the Afrodystopic episteme?" he writes. This debate remains open.

Thanks to the six comments for which I express my thanks again, it looks like several leads appear that may be put to use to carry on the study of the unfathomable object that is witchcraft/sorcery: an ethnography of enunciation, and hermeneutics of discourse, popular and scholarly epistemologies of human incompleteness, – whether African, European, Asiatic of other –, an anthropology of the historical subject as against the individual. Whatever the case, this contradictory debate will have been useful if it encourages scholars to exercise a modicum of caution and sobriety as regards this unusual object and the surface it occupies in the public space.

Printed in the United States
By Bookmasters